DOVER · THRIFT · EDITIONS

Great Speeches by Mark Twain

EDITED BY
BOB BLAISDELL

DOVER PUBLICATIONS, INC.
Mineola, New York

DOVER THRIFT EDITIONS

GENERAL EDITOR: MARY CAROLYN WALDREP
EDITOR OF THIS VOLUME: SUZANNE E. JOHNSON

Bibliographical Note
Great Speeches by Mark Twain is a new work, first published by Dover Publications, Inc., in 2013.

International Standard Book Number
ISBN-13: 978-0-486-49879-9
ISBN-10: 0-486-49879-4

Manufactured in the United States by Courier Corporation
49879401
www.doverpublications.com

Introduction

THIS IS THE FUNNIEST collection of Twain's humor in existence, which makes it the funniest collection of American humor and absolutely the funniest collection of speeches ever assembled. (There's no proof of those claims except in the pudding, so go ahead and skip to the speeches.) I own the 25-volume "National Edition" of Twain's work (published in 1899), so I didn't know of Twain's speeches as a separate volume until I began assembling a volume of his wit and wisdom. Upon discovering *Mark Twain's Speeches,* the 1910 posthumous collection introduced by his friend William Dean Howells, I realized it would be possible to assemble a complete volume of wit and hilarity from it alone: "As to age, the fact that I am nearly seventy-two years old does not clearly indicate how old I am, because part of every day—it is with me as with you—you try to describe your age, and you cannot do it. Sometimes you are only fifteen; sometimes you are twenty-five. It is very seldom in a day that I am seventy-two years old. I am older now sometimes than I was when I used to rob orchards; a thing which I would not do today—if the orchards were watched."[1]

Howells, feeling obliged to apologize for the speeches not giving us the experience of witnessing Twain in the flesh, or perhaps simply missing him for his own sake, remarks: "These speeches will address themselves to the minds and hearts of those who read them, but not with the effect they had with those who heard them; Clemens himself would have said, not with half the effect."[2] Supposedly, without the real-time comic pauses and emphatic accents, the speeches are shells. No apologies needed! Twain does not need an interpreter, only a reader. We know he prepared the speeches for performance, we know he adapted and modified even his liveliest passages from his books for the stage. No writer ever had a finer ear for nineteenth-century male

1. "The Savage Club Dinner." See page 155 of this volume.
2. William Dean Howells. Introduction. *Mark Twain's Speeches.* New York: Harper and Brothers. 1910.

American speech, so we cannot *help* hearing Twain in the flesh, as, in speech after speech, he plays himself playing the clown playing the wise man: "I have in mind a poem just now which is familiar to you all, familiar to everybody. And what an inspiration that was, and how instantly the present toast recalls the verses to all our minds when the most noble, the most gracious, the purest, and sweetest of all poets says: 'Woman! O woman!—er—Wom—' However, you remember the lines; and you remember how feelingly, how daintily, how almost imperceptibly the verses raise up before you, feature by feature, the ideal of a true and perfect woman; and how, as you contemplate the finished marvel, your homage grows into worship of the intellect that could create so fair a thing out of mere breath, mere words. And you call to mind now, as I speak, how the poet, with stern fidelity to the history of all humanity, delivers this beautiful child of his heart and his brain over to the trials and sorrows that must come to all, sooner or later, that abide in the earth, and how the pathetic story culminates in that apostrophe—so wild, so regretful, so full of mournful retrospection. The lines run thus: Alas!—alas!—a—alas! ——Alas! ———alas!' —and so on. I do not remember the rest; but, taken together, it seems to me that poem is the noblest tribute to woman that human genius has ever brought forth—and I feel that if I were to talk hours I could not do my great theme completer or more graceful justice than I have now done in simply quoting that poet's matchless words."[3]

These short speeches, refined by Twain through performance, seem so spontaneous and natural because he worked very hard to cultivate the art of artlessness, about which he explained: "I do that kind of speech (I mean an offhand speech), and do it well, and make no mistake in such a way to deceive the audience completely and make that audience believe it is an impromptu speech—that is art."[4] At dinners, where he knew he would be called on to make a toast, he liked to play off a topic an earlier speaker had raised. The ease with which he started from any old angle was just another professional deception. In his early days, having been a newspaper man, he knew how easy it was to botch a quotation, especially amid an uproar of laughter, so he used to distribute copies of his speeches beforehand.[5] They were his

---

3. "The Ladies." See page 10 of this volume.
4. "To the Whitefriars." See page 53 of this volume.
5. "I used to begin about a week ahead, and write out my impromptu speech and get it by heart. Then I brought it to the New England dinner printed on a piece of paper in my pocket, so that I could pass it to the reporters all cut and dried, and in order to do an impromptu speech as it should be done you have to indicate the places for pauses and hesitations. I put them all in it. And then you want the applause in the right places." *Ibid.*

painstakingly careless-seeming words and he wanted them recorded correctly. Some audience members believed in his apparent spontaneity so much that they wondered why he hadn't seemed to prepare, why he had bumbled along from subject to subject, rattling off absurd stories as if off the top of his head. Twain, like Charles Dickens, was a born actor and performer, and despite that he and Dickens were two of the very greatest writers of English of the century, they both modified their own writing for the stage. What they left us of their staged pieces shows us they also wrote for the ear that our eyes on the pages of their speeches can hear.

In his presentation of himself as a sidetracked muser, Twain has prepared us for the manners and methods of many of the greatest American comedians of the twentieth century, among them Groucho Marx, W. C. Fields, Jack Benny, Bill Cosby, and Richard Pryor. Disappointing our expectations for logical progression, and gratifying us with continual amusement, his misdirections and faltering manner disarmed his listeners and created suspense—does Twain know what he's about to say? He did know and he also knew the dreariness of 99 percent of the world's speeches, the canned sentiments, the puffery and platitudes, which he continually pulled the rug out from under. Many of his speeches dramatize a cloudy-headed or pompous fool thinking out loud:

> Our children—yours—and—mine. They seem like little things to talk about—our children, but little things often make up the sum of human life—that's a good sentence. I repeat it, little things often produce great things. Now, to illustrate, take Sir Isaac Newton—I presume some of you have heard of Mr. Newton. Well, once when Sir Isaac Newton—a mere lad—got over into the man's apple orchard—I don't know what he was doing there—I didn't come all the way from Hartford to q-u-e-s-t-i-o-n Mr. Newton's honesty—but when he was there—in the main orchard—he saw an apple fall and he was a-t-t-racted toward it, and that led to the discovery—not of Mr. Newton—but of the great law of *attraction* and gravitation.
>
> And there was once another great discoverer—I've forgotten his name, and I don't remember what he discovered, but I know it was something very important, and I hope you will all tell your children about it when you get home.[6]

No matter the occasion, whether for "education" or for fundraising for the relief of victims of manmade and natural disasters (the

---

6. "Our Children and Great Discoveries." See page 42 of this volume.

Galveston hurricane, the San Francisco earthquake and fire, the Russian pogroms), Twain saw his job was to amuse. Howells, however, was so nervous about the frivolity (the humor!) of his friend's speeches that he quoted Twain's own disclaimer to a collection of comic stories: "If I were to sell the reader a barrel of molasses, and he, instead of sweetening his substantial dinner with the same at judicious intervals, should eat the entire barrel at one sitting, and then abuse me for making him sick, I would say that he deserved to be made sick for not knowing any better how to utilize the blessings this world affords. And if I sell to the reader this volume of nonsense, and he, instead of seasoning his graver reading with a chapter of it now and then, when his mind demands such relaxation, unwisely overdoses himself with several chapters of it at a single sitting, he will deserve to be nauseated, and he will have nobody to blame but himself if he is. There is no more sin in publishing an entire volume of nonsense than there is in keeping a candy-store with no hardware in it. It lies wholly with the customer whether he will injure himself by means of either, or will derive from them the benefits which they will afford him if he uses their possibilities judiciously."[7] But why not read them all up in one gulp, at a single sitting? The American critic Marvin Mudrick observed: "The study of literature is not the study of religion. The significance of reading—I mean the *reason* you read is to be entertained. And there is a sense in which you always have to have excess before you can have sufficiency. So in order to know what reading is like, you in effect have to read to excess, you have to read overmuch."[8]

The nineteenth century represents the glory days of lecturing; authors and public figures toured the world, from big cities to back waters, and spoke to thousands upon thousands of listeners on topics great and small. Twain helped create an international taste for American humor; he certainly created his own audience. The thirty-year-old journalist began his lecturing career in 1866 in San Francisco, which he described several years later (allow for tall-taling) in *Roughing It*: "I was home again, in San Francisco, without means and without employment. I tortured my brain for a saving scheme of some kind, and at last a public lecture occurred to me! I sat down and wrote one, in a fever of hopeful anticipation. I showed it to several friends, but they all shook their heads. They said nobody would come to hear me, and I would make a humiliating failure of it." He rented out a new opera house and borrowed money to advertise and entreated friends and shills in the

7. *Mark Twain's Speeches.* 1910. Howells is quoting from the Preface to the English edition of *Mark Twain's Sketches.*
8. *Mudrick Transcribed: Classes and Talks by Marvin Mudrick.* Edited by Lance Kaplan. Santa Barbara. 1989. 17.

audience to laugh it up. Once on the stage, he says, "The tumult in my heart and brain and legs continued a full minute before I could gain any command over myself. Then I recognized the charity and the friendliness in the faces before me, and little by little my fright melted away, and I began to talk. Within three or four minutes I was comfortable, and even content. My three chief allies, with three auxiliaries, were on hand, in the parquette, all sitting together, all armed with bludgeons, and all ready to make an onslaught upon the feeblest joke that might show its head. And whenever a joke did fall, their bludgeons came down and their faces seemed to split from ear to ear."[9]

Twain regularly quit public-speaking "forever," but couldn't get enough of it. After a financial disaster in the 1890s that left him bankrupt, he did a two-year around-the-world lecture tour that helped him resolve his debts and resolve that he would never again lecture *for money*.

Of the nearly two hundred surviving speeches or excerpts Professor Paul Fatout collected in 1976, I have chosen the fifty-five best and funniest (only seven of which[10] are not from the original 1910 collection that was published only two months after Twain died) and arranged them in chronological order.[11] For the most part I have used the identifying notational titles slapped on by Twain, Howells or F. A. Nast; they are not a writer's but a performer's titles, linked usually to the date, occasion or the toast prompt (e.g. "Accident Insurance—Etc."; "At the Daly Theatre"; "Literature"). Though a wonderful treasury, *Mark Twain's Speeches* was a rush job compiled by Nast (whose name does not appear anywhere in the volume), with "Fourth of July" speeches thrown together in a heap at the end, "Women," as a topic, shunted together early on, and many dates either overlooked or mistaken. In the nearly exhaustive *Mark Twain Speaking*, Fatout's only misstep, not counting the debatable decision to make "composite" versions of the speeches (many had multiple versions), is to doubt our ability to hear and catch Twain's voice: "however faithfully reproduced the words of a speech, any version published in the hard light of the morning-after failed to catch rhythm, emphasis and facial expressions—what [Twain] called the unspoken implications and soul of the delivery."[12] But we readers have always had the best stage in the world, our own mind's eye and ear. We have Mark Twain in our heads and the soul of his delivery breathing through us every time we laugh.

---

9. Mark Twain. *Roughing It.* Chapter 78.
10. The sources of these seven speeches have been noted at the end of those selections.
11. Which order Paul Fatout, in *Mark Twain Speaking*, doggedly tracked for all of us editors following him.
12. Paul Fatout. *Mark Twain Speaking.* Iowa City: University of Iowa Press. 1976. xx.

★ ★ ★

Do we really need a review of Twain's life story? Don't we all know it, more or less? As I consider these questions, Twain, from his grave in Elmira, upstate New York, cries "Malarkey!":

> The battle of Waterloo was fought on the 18th of June, 1815. I do not state this fact as a reminder to the reader, but as news to him. For a forgotten fact *is* news when it comes again. Writers of books have the fashion of whizzing by vast and renowned historical events with the remark, "The details of this tremendous episode are too familiar to the reader to need repeating here." They know that that is not true. It is a low kind of flattery. They know that the reader has forgotten every detail of it, and that nothing of the tremendous event is left in his mind but a vague and formless luminous smudge. Aside from the desire to flatter the reader, they have another reason for making the remark—two reasons, indeed. They do not remember the details themselves, and do not want the trouble of hunting them up and copying them out; also, they are afraid that if they search them out and print them they will be scoffed at by the book-reviewers for retelling those worn old things which are familiar to everybody. They should not mind the reviewer's jeer; *he* doesn't remember any of the worn old things until the book which he is reviewing has retold them to him.[13]

So instead of pretending I know and you know Twain's biography off the tops of our heads, I'll take the trouble of hunting up some details and offer the briefest outline.

That is, that he was born Samuel Clemens on November 30, 1835, in Florida, Missouri; Twain remained devoted to his mother Jane her whole long life; we certainly remember he was raised in Hannibal, Missouri, on the banks of the Mississippi, and probably, courtesy of Tom Sawyer and Huck Finn, we imagine we know how young Sam and his brothers caroused; it's easy to forget (I did, anyway) that Twain's father died when he was eleven or that as a teenager Twain worked at his older brother Orion's newspaper; we probably all remember that Twain became a riverboat pilot, from which calling his pen-name derived; it was during the Civil War that he did a week or two of training in a Confederate troop, and then set out with brother Orion to Nevada, which adventure Twain wrote up with his usual comedy and thoroughness in *Roughing It*. We have to know that Twain spun along from the 1860s to the '90s composing some of American litera-

---

13. Mark Twain. *Following the Equator: A Journey Around the World.* 1897.

ture's best and most famous humorous stories, travel books, novels and children's books, and we won't be surprised to recall he became world famous for his writing and lecturing. His personal life might not ring so many bells, but in 1870 he married a woman from upstate New York named Olivia; when he wasn't traveling around the world, he and Olivia and their kids usually lived in Connecticut. I always forget that he had four children, his only son dying as an infant; it pangs me when I remind myself that while Twain was on his bankruptcy-alleviating lecture tour in Europe his oldest and favorite daughter died. I have it in my bones how hard it is to read Twain's letters, because he became so excited by money-making schemes and almost always lost out; only when he gave up trying to make a financial killing does it seem he became plenty comfortable. His autobiography has made him a bestseller a hundred years after his death, so we most of us know he spent the last ten years of his life dictating that giant wandering book; as an old man he stopped driving himself too hard, except when he needed to get over one grief or another; his wife died in 1904; another daughter died shortly before he did; he attended many dinners and fundraisers, where he made many of these speeches, and when he wasn't working on his autobiography he was composing rather depressing satires of American life and religion. He died at age 74 in 1910, but his kindest, funniest mode—public speaking—never seemed to have left him.

Even in 1909, with his heart giving out, he was still able to keep the jokes coming. At a girls school graduation on June 9, he offered them and all of us profound advice on the perils of excess: "First, girls, don't smoke—that is, don't smoke to excess. I am seventy-three and a half years old, and have been smoking seventy-three of them. But I never smoke to excess—that is, I smoke in moderation, only one cigar at a time. Second, don't drink—that is, don't drink to excess. Third, don't marry—I mean, to excess."[14] Now, let us read these speeches—I mean, to excess.

—*Bob Blaisdell*
New York City
June 2012

---

14. *Mark Twain's Speeches.* New York: Harper and Brothers. 1910. 107.

Contents

WOMAN—AN OPINION

Washington, D.C., January 11, 1868

After the banquet's twelfth toast ("Woman—The pride of any profession, and the jewel of ours"), Twain rose to speak to the Washington Correspondents Club.

Mr. President, I do not know why I should be singled out to receive the greatest distinction of the evening—for so the office of replying to the toast of woman has been regarded in every age. I do not know why I have received this distinction, unless it be that I am a trifle less homely than the other members of the club. But be this as it may, Mr. President, I am proud of the position, and you could not have chosen any one who would have accepted it more gladly, or labored with a heartier good-will to do the subject justice than I—because, sir, I love the sex. I love all the women, irrespective of age or color.

Human intellect cannot estimate what we owe to woman, sir. She sews on our buttons; she mends our clothes; she ropes us in at the church fairs; she confides in us; she tells us whatever she can find out about the little private affairs of the neighbors; she gives us good advice, and plenty of it; she soothes our aching brows; she bears our children—ours as a general thing. In all relations of life, sir, it is but a just and graceful tribute to woman to say of her that she is a brick.

Wheresoever you place woman, sir—in whatever position or estate—she is an ornament to the place she occupies, and a treasure to the world. *[Here Mr. Clemens paused, looked inquiringly at his hearers, and remarked that the applause should come in at this point. It came in. He resumed his eulogy.]* Look at Cleopatra!—look at Desdemona!—look at Florence Nightingale!—look at Joan of Arc!—look at Lucretia Borgia! *[Disapprobation expressed.]* Well *[said Mr. Clemens, scratching his head, doubtfully]*, suppose we let Lucretia slide. Look at Joyce Heth!—Look at Mother Eve! You need not look at her unless you want to, but *[said Mr. Clemens, reflectively, after a pause]* Eve was ornamental, sir—particularly before the fashions changed. I repeat, sir, look at the illustrious names

1

of history. Look at the Widow Machree!—Look at Lucy Stone!—look at Elizabeth Cady Stanton!—Look at George Francis Train! And, sir, I say it with bowed head and deepest veneration—look at the mother of Washington! She raised a boy that could not tell a lie—could not tell a lie! But he never had any chance. It might have been different if he had belonged to the Washington Newspaper Correspondents' Club.

I repeat, sir, that in whatever position you place a woman she is an ornament to society and a treasure to the world. As a sweetheart, she has few equals and no superiors; as a cousin, she is convenient; as a wealthy grandmother with an incurable distemper, she is precious; as a wet-nurse, she has no equal among men.

What, sir, would the people of the earth be without woman? They would be scarce, sir, almighty scarce.

Then let us cherish her; let us protect her; let us give her our support, our encouragement, our sympathy, ourselves—if we get a chance.

But, jesting aside, Mr. President, woman is lovable, gracious, kind of heart, beautiful—worthy of all respect, of all esteem, of all deference. Not any here will refuse to drink her health right cordially in this bumper of wine, for each and every one has personally known, and loved, and honored the very best one of them all—his own mother.

THE OLDEST OF THE REPUBLICS—VENICE: PAST AND PRESENT

San Francisco, July 2, 1868

Twain created a stir for his lecture by publishing in San Francisco newspapers made-up letters of protest against his lecturing. The Mercantile Library Building "was well filled with admirers," according to a reporter for the Daily Alta California *newspaper. Only this excerpt survives.*

Ladies and Gentlemen: If anyone in San Francisco has a just right this evening to feel gratified—more, to feel proud—it is I, who stand before you. The compliment of your attendance here I thoroughly appreciate. It is a greater compliment than I really deserve, perhaps—but for that matter I have always been rather better treated in San Francisco than I actually deserved. I am willing to say that.

I appreciate your attendance here tonight all the more because there was such a wide-spread, such a furious, such a determined opposition to my lecturing upon this occasion. Pretty much the entire community wrote petitions imploring me not to lecture—to forbear—to have compassion upon a persecuted people. I have never had such a unanimous call to—to—to leave, before. But I resisted, and am here; and I am glad that I am privileged to address a full house, instead of having to pour out this cataract of wisdom upon empty benches.

I do not exactly propose to instruct you this evening, but rather to tell you a good many things which you have known very well before, no doubt, but which may have grown dim in your memories—for the multifarious duties and annoyances of daily life are apt to drive from our minds a large part of what we learn, and that knowledge is of little use which we cannot recall. So I simply propose to refresh your memories. I trust this will be considered sufficient apology for making this lecture somewhat didactic. I don't know what didactic means, but it is a good, high-sounding word, and I wish to use it, meaning no harm whatever.

SOURCE: *The (San Francisco) Daily Alta California*. July 3, 1868.

ABOUT LONDON

London, c. September 22, 1872

Twain spoke to the Savage Club, where he was guest of honor.

It affords me sincere pleasure to meet this distinguished club, a club which has extended its hospitalities and its cordial welcome to so many of my countrymen. I hope you will excuse these clothes. I am going to the theater; that will explain these clothes. I have other clothes than these. Judging human nature by what I have seen of it, I suppose that the customary thing for a stranger to do when he stands here is to make a pun on the name of this club, under the impression, of course, that he is the first man that that idea has occurred to. It is a credit to our human nature, not a blemish upon it; for it shows that underlying all our depravity (and God knows and you know we are depraved enough) and all our sophistication, and untarnished by them, there is a sweet germ of innocence and simplicity still. When a stranger says to me, with a glow of inspiration in his eye, some gentle, innocuous little thing about "Twain and one flesh," and all that sort of thing, I don't try to crush that man into the earth—no. I feel like saying: "Let me take you by the hand, sir; let me embrace you; I have not heard that pun for weeks." We will deal in palpable puns. We will call parties named King "Your Majesty," and we will say to the Smiths that we think we have heard that name before somewhere. Such is human nature. We cannot alter this. It is God that made us so for some good and wise Purpose. Let us not repine. But though I may seem strange, may seem eccentric, I mean to refrain from punning upon the name of this club, though I could make a very good one if I had time to think about it—a week.

I cannot express to you what entire enjoyment I find in this first visit to this prodigious metropolis of yours. Its wonders seem to me to be limitless. I go about as in a dream—as in a realm of enchantment—where many things are rare and beautiful, and all things are strange and marvelous. Hour after hour I stand—I stand spellbound, as it were—and gaze upon the statuary in Leicester Square.

4

I visit the mortuary effigies of noble old Henry VIII., and Judge Jeffreys, and the preserved gorilla, and try to make up my mind which of my ancestors I admire the most. I go to that matchless Hyde Park and drive all around it, and then I start to enter it at the Marble Arch— and am induced to "change my mind." It is a great benefaction—is Hyde Park. There, in his hansom cab, the invalid can go—the poor, sad child of misfortune—and insert his nose between the railings, and breathe the pure, health-giving air of the country and of heaven. And if he is a swell invalid, who isn't obliged to depend upon parks for his country air, he can drive inside—if he owns his vehicle. I drive round and round Hyde Park, and the more I see of the edges of it the more grateful I am that the margin is extensive.

And I have been to the Zoological Gardens. What a wonderful place that is! I never have seen such a curious and interesting variety of wild animals in any garden before—except "Mabille." I never believed before there were so many different kinds of animals in the world as you can find there—and I don't believe it yet. I have been to the British Museum. I would advise you to drop in there some time when you have nothing to do—for five minutes—if you have never been there. It seems to me the noblest monument that this nation has yet erected to her greatness. I say to her, our greatness—as a nation. True, she has built other monuments, and stately ones, as well; but these she has uplifted in honor of two or three colossal demigods who have stalked across the world's stage, destroying tyrants and delivering nations, and whose prodigies will still live in the memories of men ages after their monuments shall have crumbled to dust—I refer to the Wellington and Nelson monuments, and—the Albert memorial.

The library at the British Museum I find particularly astounding. I have read there hours together, and hardly made an impression on it. I revere that library. It is the author's friend. I don't care how mean a book is, it always takes one copy. And then every day that author goes there to gaze at that book, and is encouraged to go on in the good work. And what a touching sight it is of a Saturday afternoon to see the poor, care-worn clergymen gathered together in that vast reading-room cabbaging sermons for Sunday. You will pardon my referring to these things. Everything in this monster city interests me, and I cannot keep from talking, even at the risk of being instructive.

People here seem always to express distances by parables. To a stranger it is just a little confusing to be so parabolic—so to speak. I collar a citizen, and I think I am going to get some valuable information out of him. I ask him how far it is to Birmingham, and he says it is twenty-one shillings and sixpence. Now we know that doesn't help a man who is trying to learn. I find myself downtown somewhere, and

I want to get some sort of idea where I am—being usually lost when alone—and I stop a citizen and say: "How far is it to Charing Cross?" "Shilling fare in a cab," and off he goes. I suppose if I were to ask a Londoner how far it is from the sublime to the ridiculous, he would try to express it in coin.

But I am trespassing upon your time with these geological statistics and historical reflections. I will not longer keep you from your orgies. 'Tis a real pleasure for me to be here, and I thank you for it. The name of the Savage Club is associated in my mind with the kindly interest and the friendly offices which you lavished upon an old friend of mine who came among you a stranger, and you opened your English hearts to him and gave him welcome and a home—Artemus Ward. Asking that you will join me, I give you his memory.

AMERICANS AND THE ENGLISH

London, July 4, 1873

At a "meeting of Americans" on Independence Day, Twain delivered an address.

Mr. Chairman and Ladies and Gentlemen,

I thank you for the compliment which has just been tendered me, and to show my appreciation of it I will not afflict you with many words. It is pleasant to celebrate in this peaceful way, upon this old mother soil, the anniversary of an experiment which was born of war with this same land so long ago, and wrought out to a successful issue by the devotion of our ancestors. It has taken nearly a hundred years to bring the English and Americans into kindly and mutually appreciative relations, but I believe it has been accomplished at last. It was a great step when the two last misunderstandings were settled by arbitration instead of cannon. It is another great step when England adopts our sewing-machines without claiming the invention—as usual. It was another when they imported one of our sleeping-cars the other day. And it warmed my heart more than I can tell, yesterday, when I witnessed the spectacle of an Englishman ordering an American sherry cobbler of his own free will and accord—and not only that but with a great brain and a level head reminding the barkeeper not to forget the strawberries. With a common origin, a common language, a common literature, a common religion, and common drinks, what is longer needful to the cementing of the two nations together in a permanent bond of brotherhood?

This is an age of progress, and ours is a progressive land. A great and glorious land, too—a land which has developed a Washington, a Franklin, a William M. Tweed, a Longfellow, a Motley, a Jay Gould, a Samuel C. Pomeroy, a recent Congress which has never had its equal (in some respects), and a United States Army which conquered sixty Indians in eight months by tiring them out—which is much better than uncivilized slaughter, God knows. We have a criminal jury system

7

which is superior to any in the world and its efficiency is only marred by the difficulty of finding twelve men every day who don't know anything and can't read. And I may observe that we have an insanity plea that would have saved Cain. I think I can say, and say with pride, that we have some legislatures that bring higher prices than any in the world.

I refer with effusion to our railway system, which contents to let us live, though it might do the opposite, being our owners. It only destroyed three thousand and seventy lives last year by collisions, and twenty-seven thousand two hundred and sixty by running over heedless and unnecessary people at crossings. The companies seriously regretted the killing of these thirty thousand people, and went so far as to pay for some of them—voluntarily, of course, for the meanest of us would not claim that we possess a court treacherous enough to enforce a law against a railway company. But, thank Heaven, the railway companies are generally disposed to do the right and kindly thing without compulsion. I know of an instance which greatly touched me at the time. After an accident the company sent home the remains of a dear distant old relative of mine in a basket, with the remark, "Please state what figure you hold him at—and return the basket." Now there couldn't be anything friendlier than that.

But I must not stand here and brag all night. However, you won't mind a body bragging a little about his country on the Fourth of July. It is a fair and legitimate time to fly the eagle. I will say only one more word of brag—and a hopeful one. It is this. We have a form of government which gives each man a fair chance and no favor. With us no individual is born with a right to look down upon his neighbor and hold him in contempt. Let such of us as are not dukes find our consolation in that. And we may find hope for the future in the fact that as unhappy as is the condition of our political morality today, England has risen up out of a far fouler since the days when Charles I ennobled courtesans and all political place was a matter of bargain and sale. There is hope for us yet.

★ ★ ★

At least the above is the speech which I was going to make, but our minister, General Schenck, presided, and after the blessing, got up and made a great, long, inconceivably dull harangue, and wound up by saying that inasmuch as speech-making did not seem to exhilarate the guests much, all further oratory would be dispensed with during the evening, and we could just sit and talk privately to our elbow-neighbors and have a good, sociable time. It is known that in consequence of that remark forty-four perfected speeches died in the womb. The depression, the gloom, the solemnity that reigned over the banquet from that time forth will be a lasting memory with many that were there. By that one thoughtless remark General Schenck lost forty-four of the best friends he had in England. More than one said that night: "And this is the sort of person that is sent to represent us in a great sister empire!"

THE LADIES

London, c. November 1873

In England to give lectures related to his travel book Roughing It, *Twain spoke at the Scottish Corporation of London's anniversary festival.*

I am proud, indeed, of the distinction of being chosen to respond to this especial toast, to "The Ladies," or to women if you please, for that is the preferable term, perhaps; it is certainly the older, and therefore the more entitled to reverence. I have noticed that the Bible, with that plain, blunt honesty which is such a conspicuous characteristic of the Scriptures, is always particular to never refer to even the illustrious mother of all mankind as a "lady," but speaks of her as a woman. It is odd, but you will find it is so.

I am peculiarly proud of this honor, because I think that the toast to women is one which, by right and by every rule of gallantry, should take precedence of all others—of the army, of the navy, of even royalty itself—perhaps, though the latter is not necessary in this day and in this land, for the reason that, tacitly, you do drink a broad general health to all good women when you drink the health of the Queen of England and the Princess of Wales. I have in mind a poem just now which is familiar to you all, familiar to everybody. And what an inspiration that was, and how instantly the present toast recalls the verses to all our minds when the most noble, the most gracious, the purest, and sweetest of all poets says:

> Woman! O woman!—er—
> Wom—

However, you remember the lines; and you remember how feelingly, how daintily, how almost imperceptibly the verses raise up before you, feature by feature, the ideal of a true and perfect woman; and how, as you contemplate the finished marvel, your homage grows into worship of the intellect that could create so fair a thing out of mere breath, mere words. And you call to mind now, as I speak, how the poet, with stern

fidelity to the history of all humanity, delivers this beautiful child of
his heart and his brain over to the trials and sorrows that must come to
all, sooner or later, that abide in the earth, and how the pathetic story
culminates in that apostrophe—so wild, so regretful, so full of mournful retrospection. The lines run thus:

> Alas!—alas!—a—alas!
> ——Alas! ————alas!

—and so on. I do not remember the rest; but, taken together, it seems
to me that poem is the noblest tribute to woman that human genius
has ever brought forth—and I feel that if I were to talk hours I could
not do my great theme completer or more graceful justice than I have
now done in simply quoting that poet's matchless words. The phases
of the womanly nature are infinite in their variety. Take any type of
woman, and you shall find in it something to respect, something to
admire, something to love. And you shall find the whole joining you
heart and hand.

Who was more patriotic than Joan of Arc? Who was braver? Who
has given us a grander instance of self-sacrificing devotion? Ah! you
remember, you remember well, what a throb of pain, what a great
tidal wave of grief swept over us all when Joan of Arc fell at Waterloo.
Who does not sorrow for the loss of Sappho, the sweet singer of Israel?
Who among us does not miss the gentle ministrations, the softening
influences, the humble piety of Lucretia Borgia? Who can join in the
heartless libel that says woman is extravagant in dress when he can
look back and call to mind our simple and lowly mother Eve arrayed
in her modification of the Highland costume? Sir, women have been
soldiers, women have been painters, women have been poets. As long
as language lives the name of Cleopatra will live. And not because she
conquered George III—but because she wrote those divine lines:

> Let dogs delight to bark and bite,
> For God hath made them so.

The story of the world is adorned with the names of illustrious ones
of our own sex—some of them sons of St. Andrew, too—Scott, Bruce,
Burns, the warrior Wallace, Ben Nevis—the gifted Ben Lomond, and
the great new Scotchman, Ben Disraeli. Out of the great plains of history tower whole mountain ranges of sublime women—the Queen
of Sheba, Josephine, Semiramis, Sairey Gamp; the list is endless—but I
will not call the mighty roll, the names rise up in your own memories
at the mere suggestion, luminous with the glory of deeds that cannot
die, hallowed by the loving worship of the good and the true of all
epochs and all climes. Suffice it for our pride and our honor that we

in our day have added to it such names as those of Grace Darling and Florence Nightingale.

Woman is all that she should be—gentle, patient, long-suffering, trustful, unselfish, full of generous impulses. It is her blessed mission to comfort the sorrowing, plead for the erring, encourage the faint of purpose, succor the distressed, uplift the fallen, befriend the friendless—in a word, afford the healing of her sympathies and a home in her heart for all the bruised and persecuted children of misfortune that knock at its hospitable door. And when I say, God bless her, there is none among us who has known the ennobling affection of a wife, or the steadfast devotion of a mother but in his heart will say, Amen!

ACCIDENT INSURANCE—ETC.

Hartford, Connecticut, October 12, 1874

Twain spoke at the Insurance Men's Banquet at Allyn House for the British insurance agent Cornelius Walford. Twain himself was, as he mentions below, a member of the board of the Hartford Accident Insurance Company.

Gentlemen,

I am glad, indeed, to assist in welcoming the distinguished guest of this occasion to a city whose fame as an insurance center has extended to all lands, and given us the name of being a quadruple band of brothers working sweetly hand in hand—the Colt's arms company making the destruction of our race easy and convenient, our life-insurance citizens paying for the victims when they pass away, Mr. Batterson perpetuating their memory with his stately monuments, and our fire-insurance comrades taking care of their hereafter. I am glad to assist in welcoming our guest—first, because he is an Englishman, and I owe a heavy debt of hospitality to certain of his fellow-countrymen; and secondly, because he is in sympathy with insurance, and has been the means of making many other men cast their sympathies in the same direction.

Certainly there is no nobler field for human effort than the insurance line of business—especially accident insurance. Ever since I have been a director in an accident-insurance company I have felt that I am a better man. Life has seemed more precious. Accidents have assumed a kindlier aspect. Distressing special providences have lost half their horror. I look upon a cripple now with affectionate interest—as an advertisement. I do not seem to care for poetry any more. I do not care for politics even agriculture does not excite me. But to me now there is a charm about a railway collision that is unspeakable.

There is nothing more beneficent than accident insurance. I have seen an entire family lifted out of poverty and into affluence by the simple boon of a broken leg. I have had people come to me on crutches, with tears in their eyes, to bless this beneficent institution. In all my experience of life, I have seen nothing so seraphic as the look that comes into a freshly mutilated man's face when he feels in his vest pocket with his remaining hand and finds his accident ticket all right. And I have seen nothing so sad as the look that came into another splintered customer's face when he found he couldn't collect on a wooden leg.

I will remark here, by way of advertisement, that that noble charity which we have named the HARTFORD ACCIDENT INSURANCE COMPANY is an institution which is peculiarly to be depended upon. A man is bound to prosper who gives it his custom. No man can take out a policy in it and not get crippled before the year is out. Now there was one indigent man who had been disappointed so often with other companies that he had grown disheartened, his appetite left him, he ceased to smile—said life was but a weariness. Three weeks ago I got him to insure with us, and now he is the brightest, happiest spirit in this land—has a good steady income and a stylish suit of new bandages every day, and travels around on a shutter.

I will say, in conclusion, that my share of the welcome to our guest is nonetheless hearty because I talk so much nonsense, and I know that I can say the same for the rest of the speakers.

THE WEATHER OF NEW ENGLAND

New York City, December 22, 1876

Twain addressed the New England Society's 71st Annual Dinner at Delmonico's Restaurant. Twain later described his wonder at the marvel of ice storms in Following the Equator: A Journey Around the World (1897).

> Who can lose it and forget it?
> Who can have it and regret it?
> Be interposer 'twixt us Twain.
> —*Merchant of Venice.*

I reverently believe that the Maker who made us all makes everything in New England but the weather. I don't know who makes that, but I think it must be raw apprentices in the weather-clerk's factory who experiment and learn how, in New England, for board and clothes, and then are promoted to make weather for countries that require a good article, and will take their custom elsewhere if they don't get it. There is a sumptuous variety about the New England weather that compels the stranger's admiration—and regret. The weather is always doing something there; always attending strictly to business; always getting up new designs and trying them on the people to see how they will go. But it gets through more business in spring than in any other season.

In the spring I have counted one hundred and thirty-six different kinds of weather inside of four-and-twenty hours. It was I that made the fame and fortune of that man that had that marvelous collection of weather on exhibition at the Centennial, that so astounded the foreigners. He was going to travel all over the world and get specimens from all the climes. I said, "Don't you do it; you come to New England on a favorable spring day." I told him what we could do in the way of style, variety, and quantity. Well, he came and he made his collection in four days. As to variety, why, he confessed that he got hundreds of kinds of weather that he had never heard of before. And as to quantity—well, after he had picked out and discarded all that was blemished in any way, he not only had weather enough, but weather to spare; weather to hire out; weather to sell; to deposit; weather to invest; weather to give to the poor.

The people of New England are by nature patient and forbearing, but there are some things which they will not stand. Every year they kill a lot of poets for writing about "Beautiful Spring." These are generally casual visitors, who bring their notions of spring from somewhere else, and cannot, of course, know how the natives feel about spring. And so the first thing they know the opportunity to inquire how they feel has permanently gone by. Old Probabilities has a mighty reputation for accurate prophecy, and thoroughly well deserves it. You take up the paper and observe how crisply and confidently he checks off what today's weather is going to be on the Pacific, down South, in the Middle States, in the Wisconsin region. See him sail along in the joy and pride of his power till he gets to New England, and then see his tail drop. *He* doesn't know what the weather is going to be in New England. Well, he mulls over it, and by-and-by he gets out something about like this: Probably northeast to southwest winds, varying to the southward and westward and eastward, and points between, high and low barometer swapping around from place to place; probable areas of rain, snow, hail, and drought, succeeded or preceded by earthquakes, with thunder and lightning. Then he jots down his postscript from his wandering mind, to cover accidents. "But it is possible that the program may be wholly changed in the mean time."

Yes, one of the brightest gems in the New England weather is the dazzling uncertainty of it. There is only one thing certain about it: you are certain there is going to be plenty of it—a perfect grand review; but you never can tell which end of the procession is going to move first. You fix up for the drought; you leave your umbrella in the house and sally out, and two to one you get drowned. You make up your mind that the earthquake is due; you stand from under, and take hold of something to steady yourself, and the first thing you know you get struck by lightning. These are great disappointments; but they can't be helped. The lightning there is peculiar; it is so convincing, that when it strikes a thing it doesn't leave enough of that thing behind for you to tell whether—

Well, you'd think it was something valuable, and a Congressman had been there. And the thunder. When the thunder begins to merely tune up and scrape and saw, and key up the instruments for the performance, strangers say, "Why, what awful thunder you have here!" But when the baton is raised and the real concert begins, you'll find that stranger down in the cellar with his head in the ash-barrel.

Now as to the size of the weather in New England—lengthways, I mean. It is utterly disproportioned to the size of that little country. Half the time, when it is packed as full as it can stick, you will see that New England weather sticking out beyond the edges and projecting around hundreds and hundreds of miles over the neighboring States. She can't hold a tenth part of her weather. You can see cracks all about where she has strained herself trying to do it. I could speak volumes about the inhuman perversity of the New England weather, but I will give but a single specimen. I like to hear rain on a tin roof. So I covered part of my roof with tin, with an eye to that luxury. Well, sir, do you think it ever rains on that tin? No, sir; skips it every time.

Mind, in this speech I have been trying merely to do honor to the New England weather—no language could do it justice. But, after all, there is at least one or two things about that weather (or, if you please, effects produced by it) which we residents would not like to part with. If we hadn't our bewitching autumn foliage, we should still have to credit the weather with one feature which compensates for all its bullying vagaries—the ice-storm: when a leafless tree is clothed with ice from the bottom to the top—ice that is as bright and clear as crystal; when every bough and twig is strung with ice-beads, frozen dew-drops, and the whole tree sparkles cold and white, like the Shah of Persia's diamond plume. Then the wind waves the branches and the sun comes out and turns all those myriads of beads and drops to prisms that glow and burn and flash with all manner of colored fires, which change and change again with inconceivable rapidity from blue to red, from red to green, and green to gold—the tree becomes a spraying fountain, a very explosion of dazzling jewels; and it stands there the acme, the climax, the supremest possibility in art or nature, of bewildering, intoxicating, intolerable magnificence. One cannot make the words too strong.

THE STORY OF A SPEECH

Boston, December 17, 1877

In honor of the poet John Greenleaf Whittier's seventieth birthday, Twain gave this speech at a dinner given by The Atlantic Monthly *at the Hotel Brunswick. Immediately following the speech is Twain's recollection of it while writing his autobiography in 1906 and then his own assessment upon rereading it.*

This is an occasion peculiarly meet for the digging up of pleasant reminiscences concerning literary folk; therefore I will drop lightly into history myself. Standing here on the shore of the Atlantic and contemplating certain of its largest literary billows, I am reminded of a thing which happened to me thirteen years ago, when I had just succeeded in stirring up a little Nevadian literary puddle myself, whose spume-flakes were beginning to blow thinly California-ward. I started an inspection tramp through the southern mines of California. I was callow and conceited, and I resolved to try the virtue of my *nom de guerre*.

I very soon had an opportunity. I knocked at a miner's lonely log cabin in the foothills of the Sierras just at nightfall. It was snowing at the time. A jaded, melancholy man of fifty, barefooted, opened the door to me. When he heard my *nom de guerre* he looked more dejected than before. He let me in—pretty reluctantly, I thought—and after the customary bacon and beans, black coffee and hot whiskey, I took a pipe. This sorrowful man had not said three words up to this time. Now he spoke up and said, in the voice of one who is secretly suffering, "You're the fourth—I'm going to move."

"The fourth what?" said I.

"The fourth littery man that has been here in twenty-four hours—I'm going to move."

"You don't tell me!" said I; "who were the others?"

"Mr. Longfellow, Mr. Emerson, and Mr. Oliver Wendell Holmes—consound the lot!"

You can easily believe I was interested. I supplicated—three hot whiskeys did the rest—and finally the melancholy miner began. Said he:

18

"They came here just at dark yesterday evening, and I let them in of course. Said they were going to the Yosemite. They were a rough lot, but that's nothing; everybody looks rough that travels afoot. Mr. Emerson was a seedy little bit of a chap, red-headed. Mr. Holmes was as fat as a balloon; he weighed as much as three hundred, and had double chins all the way down to his stomach. Mr. Longfellow was built like a prize-fighter. His head was cropped and bristly, like as if he had a wig made of hairbrushes. His nose lay straight down his face, like a finger with the end joint tilted up. They had been drinking, I could see that. And what queer talk they used! Mr. Holmes inspected this cabin, then he took me by the buttonhole, and says he:

> Through the deep caves of thought
> > I hear a voice that sings,
> Build thee more stately mansions,
> > O my soul!

"Says I, 'I can't afford it, Mr. Holmes, and moreover I don't want to.' Blamed if I liked it pretty well, either, coming from a stranger, that way. However, I started to get out my bacon and beans, when Mr. Emerson came and looked on awhile, and then he takes me aside by the buttonhole and says:

> Give me agates for my meat;
> Give me cantharids to eat;
> From air and ocean bring me foods,
> From all zones and altitudes.

"Says I, 'Mr. Emerson, if you'll excuse me, this ain't no hotel.' You see it sort of riled me—I warn't used to the ways of littery swells. But I went on a-sweating over my work, and next comes Mr. Longfellow and buttonholes me, and interrupts me. Says he:

> Honor be to Mudjekeewis!
> You shall hear how Pau-Puk-Keewis—

"But I broke in, and says I, 'Beg your pardon, Mr. Longfellow, if you'll be so kind as to hold your yawp for about five minutes and let me get this grub ready, you'll do me proud.' Well, sir, after they'd filled up I set out the jug. Mr. Holmes looks at it, and then he fires up all of a sudden and yells:

> Flash out a stream of blood-red wine!
> For I would drink to other days.

"By George, I was getting kind of worked up. I don't deny it, I was getting kind of worked up. I turns to Mr. Holmes, and says I, 'Looky

here, my fat friend, I'm a-running this shanty, and if the court knows
herself, you'll take whiskey straight or you'll go dry.' Them's the very
words I said to him. Now I don't want to sass such famous littery
people, but you see they kind of forced me. There ain't nothing unrea-
sonable 'bout me; I don't mind a passel of guests a-treadin' on my tail
three or four times, but when it comes to standing on it, it's different,
'And if the court knows herself,' I says, 'you'll take whiskey straight
or you'll go dry.' Well, between drinks they'd swell around the cabin
and strike attitudes and spout; and pretty soon they got out a greasy
old deck and went to playing euchre at ten cents a corner—on trust.
I began to notice some pretty suspicious things. Mr. Emerson dealt,
looked at his hand, shook his head, says:

> I am the doubter and the doubt—

and calmly bunched the hands and went to shuffling for a new layout.
Says he:

> They reckon ill who leave me out;
> They know not well the subtle ways I keep.
> I pass and deal *again!*

"Hang'd if he didn't go ahead and do it, too! Oh, he was a cool
one! Well, in about a minute things were running pretty tight, but all
of a sudden I see by Mr. Emerson's eye he judged he had 'em. He had
already corralled two tricks, and each of the others one. So now he
kind of lifts a little in his chair and says:

> I tire of globes and aces!—
> Too long the game is played!

—and down he fetched a right bower. Mr. Longfellow smiles as sweet
as pie and says:

> Thanks, thanks to thee, my worthy friend,
> For the lesson thou hast taught,

—and blamed if he didn't down with another right bower! Emerson
claps his hand on his bowie, Longfellow claps his on his revolver, and
I went under a bunk. There was going to be trouble; but that mon-
strous Holmes rose up, wobbling his double chins, and says he, 'Order,
gentlemen; the first man that draws, I'll lay down on him and smother
him!' All quiet on the Potomac, you bet!

"They were pretty how-come-you-so by now, and they begun to
blow. Emerson says, 'The nobbiest thing I ever wrote was "Barbara
Frietchie."' Says Longfellow, 'It don't begin with my "Biglow Papers."'
Says Holmes, 'My "Thanatopis" lays over 'em both.' They mighty near

ended in a fight. Then they wished they had some more company—and Mr. Emerson pointed to me and says:

> Is yonder squalid peasant all
> That this proud nursery could breed?

"He was a-whetting his bowie on his boot—so I let it pass. Well, sir, next they took it into their heads that they would like some music; so they made me stand up and sing 'When Johnny Comes Marching Home' till I dropped—at thirteen minutes past four this morning. That's what *I've* been through, my friend. When I woke at seven, they were leaving, thank goodness, and Mr. Longfellow had my only boots on, and his'n under his arm. Says I, 'Hold on, there, Evangeline, what are you going to do with *them?*' He says, 'Going to make tracks with 'em; because:

> Lives of great men all remind us
> We can make our lives sublime;
> And, departing, leave behind us
> Footprints on the sands of time.

As I said, Mr. Twain, you are the fourth in twenty-four hours—and I'm going to move; I ain't suited to a littery atmosphere.'"

I said to the miner, "Why, my dear sir, these were not the gracious singers to whom we and the world pay loving reverence and homage; these were impostors."

The miner investigated me with a calm eye for a while; then said he, "Ah! impostors, were they? Are you?"

I did not pursue the subject, and since then I have not traveled on my *nom de guerre* enough to hurt. Such was the reminiscence I was moved to contribute, Mr. Chairman. In my enthusiasm I may have exaggerated the details a little, but you will easily forgive me that fault, since I believe it is the first time I have ever deflected from perpendicular fact on an occasion like this.

★ ★ ★

From Mark Twain's *Autobiography*.
January 11, 1906
Answer to a letter received this morning:

> *Dear Mrs. H.,*
>   *I am forever your debtor for reminding me of that curious passage in my life. During the first year or two after it happened, I could not bear to think of it. My pain and shame were so intense, and my sense of having been an imbecile so settled, established and confirmed, that I drove*

the episode entirely from my mind—and so all these twenty-eight or twenty-nine years I have lived in the conviction that my performance of that time was coarse, vulgar, and destitute of humor. But your suggestion that you and your family found humor in it twenty-eight years ago moved me to look into the matter. So I commissioned a Boston typewriter to delve among the Boston papers of that bygone time and send me a copy of it.

It came this morning, and if there is any vulgarity about it I am not able to discover it. If it isn't innocently and ridiculously funny, I am no judge. I will see to it that you get a copy.

What I have said to Mrs. H. is true. I did suffer during a year or two from the deep humiliations of that episode. But at last, in 1888, in Venice, my wife and I came across Mr. and Mrs. A. P. C., of Concord, Massachusetts, and a friendship began then of the sort which nothing but death terminates. The C's were very bright people and in every way charming and companionable. We were together a month or two in Venice and several months in Rome, afterward, and one day that lamented break of mine was mentioned. And when I was on the point of lathering those people for bringing it to my mind when I had gotten the memory of it almost squelched, I perceived with joy that the C's were indignant about the way that my performance had been received in Boston. They poured out their opinions most freely and frankly about the frosty attitude of the people who were present at that performance, and about the Boston newspapers for the position they had taken in regard to the matter. That position was that I had been irreverent beyond belief, beyond imagination. Very well; I had accepted that as a fact for a year or two, and had been thoroughly miserable about it whenever I thought of it—which was not frequently, if I could help it. Whenever I thought of it I wondered how I ever could have been inspired to do so unholy a thing. Well, the C's comforted me, but they did not persuade me to continue to think about the unhappy episode. I resisted that. I tried to get it out of my mind, and let it die, and I succeeded. Until Mrs. H.'s letter came, it had been a good twenty-five years since I had thought of that matter; and when she said that the thing was funny I wondered if possibly she might be right. At any rate, my curiosity was aroused, and I wrote to Boston and got the whole thing copied, as above set forth.

I vaguely remember some of the details of that gathering—dimly I can see a hundred people—no, perhaps fifty—shadowy figures sitting at tables feeding, ghosts now to me, and nameless forevermore. I don't know who they were, but I can very distinctly see, seated at the grand table and facing the rest of us, Mr. Emerson, supernaturally grave, unsmiling? Mr. Whittier, grave, lovely, his beautiful spirit shining out of his face; Mr. Longfellow, with his silken white hair and his benignant face; Dr. Oliver Wendell Holmes, flashing smiles and affection and all good-fellowship everywhere like a rose-diamond whose facets are being turned toward the light first one way and then another—a charming man, and always fascinating, whether he was talking or whether he was sitting still (what he would call still, but what would be more or less motion to other people). I can see those figures with entire distinctness across this abyss of time.

One other feature is clear—Willie Winter (for these past thousand years dramatic editor of the *New York Tribune*, and still occupying that high post in his old age) was there. He was much younger then than he is now, and he showed it. It was always a pleasure to me to see Willie Winter at a banquet. During a matter of twenty years I was seldom at a banquet where Willie Winter was not also present, and where he did not read a charming poem written for the occasion. He did it this time, and it was up to standard: dainty, happy, choicely phrased, and as good to listen to as music, and sounding exactly as if it was pouring unprepared out of heart and brain.

Now at that point ends all that was pleasurable about that notable celebration of Mr. Whittier's seventieth birthday—because I got up at that point and followed Winter, with what I have no doubt I supposed would be the gem of the evening—the gay oration above quoted from the Boston paper. I had written it all out the day before and had perfectly memorized it, and I stood up there at my genial and happy and self-satisfied ease, and begin to deliver it. Those majestic guests, that row of venerable and still active volcanoes, listened, as did everybody else in the house, with attentive interest. Well, I delivered myself of—we'll say the first two hundred words of my speech. I was expecting no returns from that part of the speech, but this was not the case as regarded the rest of it. I arrived now at the dialogue: "The old miner said, 'You are the fourth, I'm going to move.' 'The fourth what?' said I. He answered, 'The fourth littery man that has been here in twenty-four hours. I am going to move.' 'Why, you don't tell me,' said I. 'Who were the others?' 'Mr. Longfellow, Mr. Emerson, Mr. Oliver Wendell Holmes, consound the lot—'"

Now, then, the house's *attention* continued, but the expression of interest in the faces turned to a sort of black frost. I wondered what the trouble was. I didn't know. I went on, but with difficulty—I struggled along, and entered upon that miner's fearful description of the bogus Emerson, the bogus Holmes, the bogus Longfellow, always hoping—but with a gradually perishing hope—that somebody would laugh, or that somebody would at least smile, but nobody did. I didn't know enough to give it up and sit down, I was too new to public speaking, and so I went on with this awful performance, and carried it clear through to the end, in front of a body of people who seemed turned to stone with horror. It was the sort of expression their faces would have worn if I had been making these remarks about the Deity and the rest of the Trinity; there is no milder way in which to describe the petrified condition and the ghastly expression of those people.

When I sat down it was with a heart which had long ceased to beat. I shall never be as dead again as I was then. I shall never be as miserable again as I was then. I speak now as one who doesn't know what the condition of things may be in the next world, but in this one I shall never be as wretched again as I was then. Howells, who was near me, tried to say a comforting word, but couldn't get beyond a gasp. There was no use—he understood the whole size of the disaster. He had good intentions, but the words froze before they could get out. It was an atmosphere that would freeze anything. If Benvenuto Cellini's salamander had been in that place he would not have survived to be put into Cellini's autobiography. There was a frightful pause. There was an awful silence, a desolating silence. Then the next man on the list had to get up—there was no help for it. That was Bishop—Bishop had just burst handsomely upon the world with a most acceptable novel, which had appeared in *The Atlantic Monthly*, a place which would make any novel respectable and any author noteworthy. In this case the novel itself was recognized as being, without extraneous help, respectable. Bishop was away up in the public favor, and he was an object of high interest, consequently there was a sort of national expectancy in the air; we may say our American millions were standing, from Maine to Texas and from Alaska to Florida, holding their breath, their lips parted, their hands ready to applaud, when Bishop should get up on that occasion, and for the first time in his life speak in public. It was under these damaging conditions that he got up to "make good," as the vulgar say. I had spoken several times before, and that is the reason why I was able to go on without dying in my tracks, as I ought to have done—but Bishop had had no experience. He was up facing those awful deities—facing those other people, those strangers-facing human beings for the first time in his life, with a speech to utter. No doubt it was well packed away in his memory, no doubt it was fresh and usable, until I had been heard from. I suppose that after that, and under the smothering pall of that dreary silence, it began to waste away and disappear out of his head like the rags breaking from the edge of a fog, and presently there wasn't any fog left. He didn't go on—he didn't last long. It was not many sentences after his first before he began to hesitate, and break, and lose his grip, and totter, and wobble, and at last he slumped down in a limp and mushy pile.

Well, the program for the occasion was probably not more than one-third finished, but it ended there. Nobody rose. The next man hadn't strength enough to get up, and everybody looked so dazed, so stupefied, paralyzed, it was impossible for anybody to do anything, or even try. Nothing could go on in that strange atmosphere. Howells mournfully, and without words, hitched himself to Bishop and me and supported us out of the room. It was very kind—he was most generous. He towed us tottering away into some room in that building, and we sat down there. I don't know what my remark was now, but I know the nature of it. It was the kind of remark you make when you know that nothing in the world can help your case. But Howells was honest—he had to say the heart-breaking things he did say: that there was no help for this calamity, this shipwreck, this cataclysm; that this was the most disastrous thing that had ever happened in anybody's history—and then he added, "That is, for you—and consider what you have done for Bishop. It is bad enough in your case, you deserve to suffer. You have committed this crime, and you deserve to have all you are going to get. But here is an innocent man. Bishop had never done you any harm, and see what you have done to him. He can never hold his head up again. The world can never look upon Bishop as being a live person. He is a corpse."

That is the history of that episode of twenty-eight years ago, which pretty nearly killed me with shame during that first year or two whenever it forced its way into my mind.

★ ★ ★

Now then, I take that speech up and examine it. As I said, it arrived this morning, from Boston. I have read it twice, and unless I am an idiot, it hasn't a single defect in it from the first word to the last. It is just as good as good can be. It is smart; it is saturated with humor. There isn't a suggestion of coarseness or vulgarity in it anywhere. What could have been the matter with that house? It is amazing, it is incredible, that they didn't shout with laughter, and those deities the loudest of them all. Could the fault have been with me? Did I lose courage when I saw those great men up there whom I was going to describe in such a strange fashion? If that happened, if I showed doubt, that can account for it, for you can't be successfully funny if you show that you are afraid of it. Well, I can't account for it, but if I had those beloved and revered old literary immortals back here now on the platform at Carnegie Hall I would take that same old speech, deliver it, word for word, and melt them till they'd run all over that stage. Oh, the fault must have been with me, it is not in the speech at all.

THE BABIES

Chicago, November 13, 1879

The Army of the Tennessee gave a banquet at the Palmer House for former United States President Ulysses S. Grant, the first commander of that army in the Civil War, and Twain's friend. After a toast to "The Babies, As they comfort us in our sorrows, let us not forget them in our festivities," Twain spoke.

I like that. We have not all had the good fortune to be ladies. We have not all been generals, or poets, or statesmen; but when the toast works down to the babies, we stand on common ground. It is a shame that for a thousand years the world's banquets have utterly ignored the baby, as if he didn't amount to anything. If you will stop and think a minute—if you will go back fifty or one hundred years to your early married life and recontemplate your first baby—you will remember that he amounted to a good deal, and even something over. You soldiers all know that when that little fellow arrived at family headquarters you had to hand in your resignation. He took entire command. You became his lackey, his mere body-servant, and you had to stand around too. He was not a commander who made allowances for time, distance, weather, or anything else. You had to execute his order whether it was possible or not. And there was only one form of marching in his manual of tactics, and that was the double-quick. He treated you with every sort of insolence and disrespect, and the bravest of you didn't dare to say a word. You could face the death-storm at Donelson and Vicksburg, and give back blow for blow; but when he clawed your whiskers, and pulled your hair, and twisted your nose, you had to take it.

When the thunders of war were sounding in your ears you set your faces toward the batteries, and advanced with steady tread; but when he turned on the terrors of his war-whoop you advanced in the other direction, and mighty glad of the chance, too. When he called for soothing-syrup, did you venture to throw out any side-remarks about certain services being unbecoming an officer and a gentleman? No. You got up and *got* it. When he ordered his pap bottle and it was not warm, did you talk back? Not you. You went to work and *warmed* it. You even descended so far in your menial office as to take a suck at that warm, insipid stuff yourself, to see if it was right—three parts water to one of milk, a touch of sugar to modify the colic, and a drop of peppermint to kill those immortal hiccoughs. I can taste that stuff yet. And how many things you learned as you went along!

Sentimental young folks still take stock in that beautiful old saying that when the baby smiles in his sleep, it is because the angels are whispering to him. Very pretty, but too thin—simply wind on the stomach, my friends. If the baby proposed to take a walk at his usual hour, two o'clock in the morning, didn't you rise up promptly and remark, with a mental addition which would not improve a Sunday-school book much, that that was the very thing you were about to propose yourself? Oh! you were under good discipline, and as you went fluttering up and down the room in your undress uniform, you not only prattled undignified baby-talk, but even tuned up your martial voices and tried to *sing!*—*Rock-a-by Baby in the Tree-top,* for instance. What a spectacle for an Army of the Tennessee! And what an affliction for the neighbors, too; for it is not everybody within a mile around that likes military music at three in the morning. And when you had been keeping this sort of thing up two or three hours, and your little velvet-head intimated that nothing suited him like exercise and noise, what did you do? You simply went on until you dropped in the last ditch.

The idea that a *baby* doesn't *amount* to anything! Why, *one* baby is just a house and a front yard full by itself. *One* baby can furnish more business than you and your whole Interior Department can attend to. He is enterprising, irrepressible, brimful of lawless activities. Do what you please, you can't make him stay on the reservation. Sufficient unto the day is one baby. As long as you are in your right mind don't you ever pray for twins. Twins amount to a permanent riot. And there ain't any real difference between triplets and an insurrection.

Yes, it was high time for a toast-master to recognize the importance of the babies. Think what is in store for the present crop! Fifty years from now we shall all be dead, I trust, and then this flag, if it still survive (and let us hope it may), will be floating over a Republic numbering 200,000,000 souls, according to the settled laws of our increase. Our present schooner of State will have grown into a political leviathan—a *Great Eastern.* The cradled babies of today will be on deck. Let them be well trained, for we are going to leave a big contract on their hands. Among the three or four million cradles now rocking in the land are some which this nation would preserve for ages as sacred things, if we could know which ones they are. In one of these cradles the unconscious Farragut of the future is at this moment teething—think of it!—and putting in a world of dead earnest, unarticulated, but perfectly justifiable profanity over it, too. In another the future renowned astronomer is blinking at the shining Milky Way with but a languid interest—poor little chap!—and wondering what has become of that other one they call the wet-nurse. In another the future great historian is lying—and doubtless will continue to lie until his earthly mission is ended. In another the future President is busying himself with no profounder problem of state than what the mischief has become of his hair so early; and in a mighty array of other cradles there are now some 60,000 future office-seekers, getting ready to furnish him occasion to grapple with that same old problem a second time.

And in still one more cradle, somewhere under the flag, the future illustrious commander-in-chief of the American armies is so little burdened with his approaching grandeurs and responsibilities as to be giving his whole strategic mind at this moment to trying to find out some way to get his big toe into his mouth—an achievement which, meaning no disrespect, the illustrious guest of this evening turned his entire attention to some fifty-six years ago; and if the child is but a prophecy of the man, there are mighty few who will doubt that he succeeded.

CANADIAN COPYRIGHT

Montreal, December 8, 1881

In Canada to try to secure copyright for his novel The Prince *and the* Pauper, *Twain gave a speech at a banquet in his honor at the Windsor Hotel. The* Montreal Gazette *reported that "The assembly was essentially a gathering of the devoted admirers of a great genius, who sought in a peculiarly English way to evince their appreciation of his literary peerage. . . . After the toasts to the Queen and the President, the latter being responded to by the Consul-General Smith, and a poem in French, composed and read by Mr. [Louis Honore] Frechette, the Poet Laureate of Canada, the toast in honor of the guest of the evening was presented and was responded to by [Twain] as follows . . . "*

That a banquet should be given to me in this ostensibly foreign land and in this great city, and that my ears should be greeted by such complimentary words from such distinguished lips, are eminent surprises to me; and I will not conceal the fact that they are also deeply gratifying. I thank you, one and all, gentlemen, for these marks of favor and friendliness; and even if I have not really or sufficiently deserved them, I assure you that I do not any the less keenly enjoy and esteem them on that account.

When a stranger appears abruptly in a country, without any apparent business there, and at an unusual season of the year, the judicious thing for him to do is to explain. This seems peculiarly necessary in my case, on account of a series of unfortunate happenings here, which followed my arrival, and which I suppose the public have felt compelled to connect with that circumstance. I would most gladly explain if I could; but I have nothing for my defense but my bare word; so I simply declare, in all sincerity, and with my hand on my heart, that I never heard of that diamond robbery till I saw it in the morning paper; and I can say with perfect truth that I never saw that box of dynamite till the Police came to inquire of me if I had any more of it.

These are mere assertions, I grant you, but they come from the lips of one who was never known to utter an untruth, except for practice,

29

and who certainly would not so stultify the traditions of an upright life as to utter one now, in a strange land, and in such a presence as this, when there is nothing to be gained by it and he does not need any practice.

I brought with me to this city a friend—a Boston publisher—but, alas, even this does not sufficiently explain these sinister mysteries; if I had brought a Toronto publisher along the case would have been different. But no, possibly not; the burglar took the diamond studs, but left the shirt; only a reformed Toronto publisher would have left that shirt.

To continue my explanation, I did not come to Canada to commit crime—this time—but to prevent it. I came here to place myself under the protection of the Canadian law and secure a copyright. I have complied with the requirements of the law; I have followed the instructions of some of the best legal minds in the city, including my own, and so my errand is accomplished, at least so far as any exertions of mine can aid that accomplishment.

This is rather a cumbersome way to fence and fortify one's property against the literary buccaneer it is true; still, if it is effective, it is a great advance upon past conditions and one to be correspondingly welcomed. It makes one hope and believe that a day will come when, in the eye of the law, literary property will be as sacred as whiskey, or any other of the necessaries of life. In this age of ours, if you steal another man's label to advertise your own brand of whiskey with, you will he heavily fined and otherwise punished for violating that trademark; if you steal the whiskey without the trademark, you go to jail; but if you could prove that the whiskey was literature, you can steal them both, and the law wouldn't say a word. It grieves me to think how far more profound and reverent a respect the law would have for literature if a body could only get drunk on it. Still the world moves; the interests of literature upon our continent are improving; let us be content and wait.

We have with us here a fellow craftsman, born on our own side of the Atlantic, who has created an epoch in this continent's literary history—an author who has earned and worthily earned and received the vast distinction of being crowned by the Academy of France. This is honor and achievement enough for the cause and the craft for one decade, assuredly.

If one may have the privilege of throwing in a personal impression or two, I may remark that my stay in Montreal and Quebec has been exceedingly pleasant, but the weather has been a good deal of a disappointment. Canada has a reputation for magnificent winter weather, and has a prophet who is bound by every sentiment of honor and duty to furnish it; but the result this time has been a mess of characterless weather, which all right-feeling Canadians are probably ashamed of.

Still, only the country is to blame; nobody has a right to blame the prophet, for this wasn't the kind of weather he promised. Well, never mind, what you lack in weather you make up in the means of grace. This is the first time I was ever in a city where you couldn't throw a brick without breaking a church window. Yet I was told that you were going to build one more. I said the scheme is good, but where are you going to find room? They said, we will build it on top of another church and use an elevator. This shows that the gift of lying is not yet dead in the land.

I suppose one must come in the summer to get the advantages of the Canadian scenery. A cabman drove me two miles up a perpendicular hill in a sleigh and showed me an admirable snowstorm from the heights of Quebec. The man was an ass; I could have seen the snowstorm as well from the hotel window and saved my money. Still, I may have been the ass myself; there is no telling; the thing is all mixed in my mind; but anyway there was an ass in the party; and I do suppose that wherever a mercenary cabman and a gifted literary character are gathered together for business, there is bound to be an ass in the combination somewhere. It has always been so in my experience; and I have usually been elected, too. But it is no matter; I would rather be an ass than a cabman, any time, except in summer time; then, with my advantages, I could be both.

I saw the Plains of Abraham, and the spot where the lamented Wolfe stood when he made the memorable remark that he would rather be the author of Gray's "Elegy" than take Quebec. But why did he say so rash a thing? It was because he supposed there was going to be international copyright. Otherwise there would be no money in it.

I was also shown the spot where Sir William Phipps stood when he said he would rather take a walk than take two Quebecs. And he took the walk. I have looked with emotion, here in your city, upon the monument which makes forever memorable the spot where Horatio Nelson did not stand when he fell. I have seen the cab which Champlain employed when he arrived overland at Quebec; I have seen the horse which Jacques Cartier rode when he discovered Montreal. I have used them both; I will never do it again. Yes, I have seen all the historical places; the localities have been pointed out to me where the scenery is warehoused for the season.

My sojourn has been to my moral and intellectual profit; I have behaved with propriety and discretion; I have meddled nowhere but in the election. But I am used to voting, for I live in a town where, if you may judge by local prints, there are only two conspicuous industries—committing burglaries and holding elections—and I like to keep my hand in, so I voted a good deal here.

Where so many of the guests are French, the propriety will be recognized of my making a portion of my speech in the beautiful language in order that I may be perfectly understood. I speak French with timidity, and not flowingly—except when excited. When using that language I have often noticed that I have hardly ever been mistaken for a Frenchman, except, perhaps, by horses; never, I believe, by people.

I had hoped that mere French construction—with English words—would answer, but this is not the case. I tried it at a gentleman's house in Quebec, and it would not work. The maid servant asked, "What would Monsieur?"

I said, "Monsieur So-and So, is he with himself?" She did not understand that either. I said, "He will desolate himself when he learns that his friend American was arrived, and he not with himself to shake him at the hand."

She did not even understand that; I don't know why, but she didn't and she lost her temper besides. Somebody in the rear called out, "Qui est donc la?" or words to that effect. She said, "C'est un fou," and shut the door on me. Perhaps she was right; but how did she ever find that out? For she had never seen me before till that moment.

But, as I have already intimated, I will close this oration with a few sentiments in the French language. I have not ornamented them, I have not burdened them with flowers or rhetoric, for, to my mind, that literature is best and most enduring which is characterized by a noble simplicity: *J'ai belle bouton d'or de mon oncle, mais je n'ai pas celui du charpentier. Si vous avez le fromage du brave menuisier, c'est bon, mais si vous ne l'avez pas, ne se desole pas, prenez le chapeau de drap noir de son beau frere malade. Tout a l'heure! Savoir faire! Qu'est ce que vous dit? Pate de fois gras! Revenons a nos moutons! Pardon, messieurs, pardonnez moi; essayant a parler la belle langue d'Ollendorf* [15] strains me more than you can possibly imagine. But I mean well, and I've done the best I could.

SOURCE: *The New York Times*. December 10, 1881

---

15. "I have beautiful buttercup of my uncle, but I do not have that of the carpenter. If you have the cheese of the brave carpenter, that's good, but if you do not have it, do not despair, take the hat of black cloth of his sick brother-in-law. Right now! Know how! What do you say? Fois gras pate! Let's return to our sheep! Pardon, gentlemen, pardon me; trying to speak the beautiful language of d'Ollendorf..." [Rough translation: BB]

PLYMOUTH ROCK AND THE PILGRIMS

Philadelphia, December 22, 1881

Twain addressed the first annual dinner of the New England Society. The president of the society teasingly introduced the famous speaker, "who was never exactly *born in New England, nor, perhaps, were any of his ancestors. He is* not *technically, therefore, of New England descent. Under the painful circumstances in which he has found himself, however, he has done the best he could—he has had all his children born there, and has made of himself a New England ancestor. He is a self-made man. More than this, and better even, in cheerful, hopeful, helpful literature he is of New England ascent. To ascend there in anything that's reasonable is difficult, for—confidentially, with the door shut—we all know that they are the brightest, ablest sons of that goodly land who never leave it, and it is among and above them that Mr. Twain has made his brilliant and permanent ascent—become a man of mark."*

I rise to protest. I have kept still for years, but really I think there is no sufficient justification for this sort of thing. What do you want to celebrate those people for?—those ancestors of yours of 1620—the *Mayflower* tribe, I mean. What do you want to celebrate *them* for? Your pardon: the gentleman at my left assures me that you are not celebrating the Pilgrims themselves, but the landing of the Pilgrims at Plymouth Rock on the 22nd of December. So you are celebrating their landing. Why, the other pretext was thin enough, but this is thinner than ever; the other was tissue, tinfoil, fish-bladder, but this is gold-leaf. Celebrating their landing! What was there remarkable about it, I would like to know? What can you be thinking of? Why, those Pilgrims had been at sea three or four months. It was the very middle of winter: it was as cold as death off Cape Cod there. Why shouldn't they come ashore? If they *hadn't* landed there would be some reason for celebrating the fact. It would have been a case of monumental leatherheadedness which the world would not willingly let die. If it had been *you*, gentlemen, you probably wouldn't have landed, but you have no shadow of right to be celebrating, in

33

your ancestors, gifts which they did not exercise, but only transmitted. Why, to be celebrating the mere landing of the Pilgrims—to be trying to make out that this most natural and simple and customary procedure was an extraordinary circumstance—a circumstance to be amazed at, and admired, aggrandized and glorified, at orgies like this for two hundred and sixty years—hang it, a horse would have known enough to land; a horse—

Pardon again; the gentleman on my right assures me that it was not merely the landing of the Pilgrims that we are celebrating, but the Pilgrims themselves. So we have struck an inconsistency here—one says it was the landing, the other says it was the Pilgrims. It is an inconsistency characteristic of your intractable and disputatious tribe, for you never agree about anything but Boston. Well, then, what do you want to celebrate those Pilgrims for? They were a mighty hard lot—you know it. I grant you, without the slightest unwillingness, that they were a deal more gentle and merciful and just than were the people of Europe of that day; I grant you that they are better than their predecessors. But what of that?—that is nothing. People always progress. You are better than your fathers and grandfathers were (this is the first time I have ever aimed a measureless slander at the departed, for I consider such things improper).

Yes, those among you who have not been in the penitentiary, if such there be, are better than your fathers and grandfathers were; but is that any sufficient reason for getting up annual dinners and celebrating you? No, by no means—by no means. Well, I repeat, those Pilgrims were a hard lot. They took good care of themselves, but they abolished everybody else's ancestors. I am a border-ruffian from the State of Missouri. I am a Connecticut Yankee by adoption. In me, you have Missouri morals, Connecticut culture; this, gentlemen, is the combination which makes the perfect man. But where are my ancestors? Whom shall I celebrate? Where shall I find the raw material?

My first American ancestor, gentlemen, was an Indian—an early Indian. Your ancestors skinned him alive, and I am an orphan. Not one drop of my blood flows in that Indian's veins today. I stand here, lone and forlorn, without an ancestor. They skinned him! I do not object to that, if they needed his fur; but alive, gentlemen—alive! They skinned him alive—and before company! That is what rankles. Think how he must have felt; for he was a sensitive person and easily embarrassed. If he had been a bird, it would have been all right, and no violence done to his feelings, because he would have been considered "dressed." But he was not a bird, gentlemen, he was a man, and probably one of the most undressed men that ever was. I ask you to put yourselves in his place. I ask it as a favor; I ask it as a tardy act of justice; I ask it in the interest of fidelity to the traditions of your ancestors; I ask it that the world may contemplate, with vision unobstructed by disguising swallow-tails and white cravats, the spectacle which the true New England Society ought to present. Cease to come to these annual orgies in this hollow modern mockery—the surplusage of raiment. Come in character; come in the summer grace, come in the unadorned simplicity, come in the free and joyous costume which your sainted ancestors provided for mine.

Later ancestors of mine were the Quakers William Robinson, Marmaduke Stevenson, *et al.* Your tribe chased them out of the country for their religion's sake; promised them death if they came back; for your ancestors had forsaken the homes they loved, and braved the perils of the sea, the implacable climate, and the savage wilderness, to acquire that highest and most precious of boons, freedom for every man on this broad continent to worship according to the dictates of his own conscience—and they were not going to allow a lot of pestiferous Quakers to interfere with it. Your ancestors broke forever the chains of political slavery, and gave the vote to every man in this wide land, excluding none!—none except those who did not belong to the orthodox church. Your ancestors—yes, they were a hard lot; but, nevertheless, they gave us religious liberty to worship as they required us to worship, and political liberty to vote as the church required; and so I the bereft one, I the forlorn one, am here to do my best to help you celebrate them right.

The Quaker woman Elizabeth Hooton was an ancestress of mine. Your people were pretty severe with her—you will confess that. But, poor thing! I believe they changed her opinions before she died, and took her into their fold; and so we have every reason to presume that when she died she went to the same place which your ancestors went to. It is a great pity, for she was a good woman. Roger Williams was an ancestor of mine. I don't really remember what your people did with him. But they banished him to Rhode Island, anyway. And then, I believe, recognizing that this was really carrying harshness to an unjustifiable extreme, they took pity on him and burned him. They were a hard lot! All those Salem witches were ancestors of mine! Your people made it tropical for them. Yes, they did; by pressure and the gallows they made such a clean deal with them that there hasn't been a witch and hardly a halter in our family from that day to this, and that is one hundred and eighty-nine years. The first slave brought into New England out of Africa by your progenitors was an ancestor of mine—for I am of a mixed breed, an infinitely shaded and exquisite Mongrel. I'm not one of your sham meerschaums that you can color in a week. No, my complexion is the patient art of eight generations. Well, in my own time, I had acquired a lot of my kin—by purchase, and swapping around, and one way and another—and was getting along very well. Then, with the inborn perversity of your lineage, you got up a war, and took them all away from me. And so, again am I bereft, again am I forlorn; no drop of my blood flows in the veins of any living being who is marketable.

O my friends, hear me and reform! I seek your good, not mine. You have heard the speeches. Disband these New England societies— nurseries of a system of steadily augmenting laudation and hosannaing, which, if persisted in uncurbed, may some day in the remote future beguile you into prevaricating and bragging. Oh, stop, stop, while you are still temperate in your appreciation of your ancestors! Hear me, I beseech you; get up an auction and sell Plymouth Rock! The Pilgrims were a simple and ignorant race. They never had seen any good rocks before, or at least any that were not watched, and so they were excusable for hopping ashore in frantic delight and clapping an iron fence around this one. But you, gentlemen, are educated; you are enlightened; you know that in the rich land of your nativity, opulent New England, overflowing with rocks, this one isn't worth, at the outside, more than thirty-five cents. Therefore, sell it, before it is injured by exposure, or at least throw it open to the patent-medicine advertisements, and let it earn its taxes.

Yes, hear your true friend—your only true friend—list to his voice. Disband these societies, hotbeds of vice, of moral decay—perpetuators of ancestral superstition. Here on this board I see water, I see milk, I see the wild and deadly lemonade. These are but steps upon the downward path. Next we shall see tea, then chocolate, then coffee—hotel coffee. A few more years—all too few, I fear—mark my words, we shall have cider! Gentlemen, pause ere it be too late. You are on the broad road which leads to dissipation, physical ruin, moral decay, gory crime and the gallows! I beseech you, I implore you, in the name of your anxious friends, in the name of your suffering families, in the name of your impending widows and orphans, stop ere it be too late. Disband these New England societies, renounce these soul-blistering saturnalia, cease from varnishing the rusty reputations of your long-vanished ancestors—the super-high-moral old iron-clads of Cape Cod, the pious buccaneers of Plymouth Rock—go home, and try to learn to behave!

However, chaff and nonsense aside, I think I honor and appreciate your Pilgrim stock as much as you do yourselves, perhaps; and I endorse and adopt a sentiment uttered by a grandfather of mine once—a man of sturdy opinions, of sincere make of mind, and not given to flattery. He said: "People may talk as they like about that Pilgrim stock, but, after all's said and done, it would be pretty hard to improve on those people; and, as for me, I don't mind coming out flat-footed and saying there ain't any way to improve on them—except having them born in Missouri!"

THE VISITING SOLDIERY

Hartford, Connecticut, October 19, 1882

At a reception for the visiting military group of Worcester Continentals, Twain delivered this short address.

Mr. Commander and Ladies and Gentlemen:

His honor, the mayor, deputes me to speak for him in answer to the toast to the city of Hartford. He is in politics a delicate situation at all times, where exceeding caution is necessary. I admire his prudence as much as I admire my own intrepidity, because, although he is not willing to answer for Hartford and to endorse it, I am.

I will back up Hartford in everything else if he will be responsible for the weather. I am sorry that the mayor imported such detestable weather as this. I wish we had had clear weather, and hope your gentlemen of Worcester won't go away without seeing our city. Now, as I am talking for Hartford, I will talk earnestly but modestly. There is much here to see—the state house, Colt's factory and the place where the Charter Oak was.

And we have an antiquity here—the East Hartford bridge. Now let me beseech you, don't go away without seeing that tunnel on stilts. You may think it a trifle, but go see it! Think what it may be to your posterity, generations hence, who come here and say, "There's that same old bridge." It is coeval with the flood and will be coexistent with the millennium.

Hartford has a larger population than any city in America except New York. It is more beautiful than any other city excepting Worcester and it is the honestest city in the world. Well, that will do for Hartford. I will rest my case there.

When asked to respond I said I would be glad to, but there were reasons why I could not make a speech. But I said I would talk. I never make a speech without getting together a lot of statistics and being instructive. The man who starts in upon a speech without preparation enters upon a sea of infelicities and troubles. I had thought of a great many things that I intended to say. In fact, nearly all these things I have heard said here tonight I had thought of. Get a man away down here on the list and he starts out empty. I was going to say something about prominent people and about the Foot Guard who have seen everything that has happened for a hundred and eleven years. Five years they fought for King George and a hundred and six for liberty. They fought a hundred and eleven years and never lost a man. And the enemy never lost a man.

What I mean, is to compliment the Foot Guards and I hope I have done so. One reason I didn't like to come here to make a prepared speech was because I have sworn off. I have reformed. I would not make a prepared speech without statistics and philosophy. The advantage of a prepared speech is that you start when you are ready and stop when you get through. If unprepared, you are all at sea, you don't know where you are. I thought to achieve brevity, but I was mistaken. A man never hangs on so long on his hind legs as when he don't know when to stop.

I once heard of a man who tried to be reformed. He tried to be brief. A number of strangers sat in a hotel parlor. One sat off to one side and said nothing. Finally all went out except one man and this dummy. Then the dummy touched this man on the shoulder and whistled. He touched again and said: "I think I have seen (whistle) you before."

"What makes you whistle?" asked the other man.

"I used to stammer, and the doctor (whistle) told me when I wanted (whistle) to speak and stammered to whistle. I did (whistle) and it cured me." (Great laughter.) So it is with a man who makes an unprepared speech. He tries to be brief and it takes him longer.

I won't detain you. We welcome you with cordial hospitality, and if you remain, we will try to furnish better weather tomorrow.

SOURCE: *Hartford Daily Courant*. October 20, 1882.

INTRODUCING GEORGE W. CABLE

Hartford, Connecticut, April 4, 1883

Twain rallied support for Cable, a Southern writer, who would soon tour with Twain as a fellow lecturer.

A complete stranger myself to Mr. Cable personally, though a great admirer of his books, I appear before you as his sponsor tonight, if he needs one. The original idea was that Mr. William Dean Howells of New York was to introduce Mr. Cable of New Orleans to the Hartford audience, when it occurred to the committee that Mr. Howells was himself a stranger to Hartford and did not know Hartford, nor did Hartford know him. So Mr. Thomas Bailey Aldrich, of Boston, was brought from Boston to introduce Mr. Howells of New York, who was to introduce Mr. Cable of New Orleans. But someone was necessary to introduce Mr. Aldrich of Boston, so Mr. Gilder of New York was asked to introduce Mr. Aldrich of Boston, who was to introduce Mr. Howells of New York, who was to introduce Mr. Cable of New Orleans. Then the same objection arose. No one knew Mr. Gilder of New York, so Mr. John Boyle O'Reilly of Boston was asked to introduce Mr. Gilder of New York, who was to introduce Mr. Aldrich of Boston, who was to introduce Mr. Howells of New York, who was to introduce Mr. Cable of New Orleans.

Once more an awful problem arose in the minds of the committee. Mr. John B. O'Reilly, of Boston, had never been in Hartford before, and only knew it as a place of five minutes for refreshments on the New Haven Railroad. The question once more arose, who would introduce Mr. O'Reilly of Boston? And for a time no proper person appeared on the horizon. After some deliberation—for the matter was getting serious—we decided to dispense with an introduction altogether, which would occupy another evening at least, and to let Cable speak for himself. I have, however, here present on the platform all these distinguished gentlemen from our suburban cities, which will account for the menagerie behind me.

And this, ladies and gentlemen of Hartford, is Mr. Cable of New Orleans.

SOURCE: Laurence Hutton. *Talks in a Library*. New York: G.P. Putnam's Sons. 1911.

OUR CHILDREN AND GREAT DISCOVERIES

New York City, April 22, 1886

Twain spoke at an Authors Club dinner at the Gilsey House.

Our children—yours—and—mine. They seem like little things to talk about—our children, but little things often make up the sum of human life—that's a good sentence. I repeat it, little things often produce great things. Now, to illustrate, take Sir Isaac Newton—I presume some of you have heard of Mr. Newton. Well, once when Sir Isaac Newton—a mere lad—got over into the man's apple orchard—I don't know what he was doing there—I didn't come all the way from Hartford to q-u-e-s-t-i-o-n Mr. Newton's honesty—but when he was there—in the main orchard—he saw an apple fall and he was *a-t-t-racted* toward it, and that led to the discovery—not of Mr. Newton—but of the great law of *attraction* and gravitation.

And there was once another great discoverer—I've forgotten his name, and I don't remember what he discovered, but I know it was something very important, and I hope you will all tell your children about it when you get home. Well, when the great discoverer was once loafin' around down in Virginia, and a-puttin' in his time flirting with Pocahontas—oh! Captain John Smith, that was the man's name—and while he and Poca were sitting in Mr. Powhatan's garden, he accidentally put his arm around her and picked something—a simple weed, which proved to be tobacco—and now we find it in every Christian family, shedding its civilizing influence broadcast throughout the whole religious community.

Now there was another great man, I can't think of his name either, who used to loaf around and watch the great chandelier in the cathedral at Pisa, which set him to thinking about the great law of gunpowder, and eventually led to the discovery of the cotton-gin.

Now, I don't say this as an inducement for our young men to loaf around like Mr. Newton and Mr. Galileo and Captain Smith, but they were once little babies two days old, and they show what little things have sometimes accomplished.

AT THE DALY THEATRE

New York City, April 13, 1887

After the theater's one hundredth performance of The Taming of the Shrew, *Twain gave the following speech, which he later rewrote and elaborated upon as part of Chapter 45 of* Following the Equator *(1897).*

I am glad to be here. This is the hardest theater in New York to get into, even at the front door. I never got in without hard work. I am glad we have got so far in at last. Two or three years ago I had an appointment to meet Mr. Daly on the stage of this theater at eight o'clock in the evening. Well, I got on a train at Hartford to come to New York and keep the appointment. All I had to do was to come to the back door of the theater on Sixth Avenue. I did not believe that; I did not believe it could be on Sixth Avenue, but that is what Daly's note said—come to that door, walk right in, and keep the appointment. It looked very easy. It looked easy enough, but I had not much confidence in the Sixth Avenue door.

Well, I was kind of bored on the train, and I bought some newspapers—New Haven newspapers—and there was not much news in them, so I read the advertisements. There was one advertisement of a bench-show. I had heard of bench-shows, and I often wondered what there was about them to interest people. I had seen bench-shows—lectured to bench-shows, in fact—but I didn't want to advertise them or to brag about them. Well, I read on a little, and learned that a bench-show was not a bench-show—but dogs, not benches at all—only dogs. I began to be interested, and as there was nothing else to do I read every bit of the advertisement, and learned that the biggest thing in this show was a St. Bernard dog that weighed one hundred and forty-five pounds. Before I got to New York I was so interested in the bench-shows that I made up my mind to go to one the first chance I got.

Down on Sixth Avenue, near where that back door might be, I began to take things leisurely. I did not like to be in too much of a hurry. There was not anything in sight that looked like a back door. The nearest approach to it was a cigar store. So I went in and bought a cigar, not too expensive, but it cost enough to pay for any information I might get and leave the dealer a fair profit. Well, I did not like to be too abrupt, to make the man think me crazy, by asking him if that was the way to Daly's Theatre, so I started gradually to lead up to the subject, asking him first if that was the way to Castle Garden. When I got to the real question, and he said he would show me the way, I was astonished.

He sent me through a long hallway, and I found myself in a back yard. Then I went through a long passageway and into a little room, and there before my eyes was a big St. Bernard dog lying on a bench. There was another door beyond and I went there, and was met by a big, fierce man with a fur cap on and coat off, who remarked, "Phwat do yez want?" I told him I wanted to see Mr. Daly. "Yez can't see Mr. Daly this time of night," he responded. I urged that I had an appointment with Mr. Daly, and gave him my card, which did not seem to impress him much. "Yez can't get in and yez can't shmoke here. Throw away that cigar. If yez want to see Mr. Daly, yez'll have to be after going to the front door and buy a ticket, and then if yez have luck and he's around that way yez may see him."

I was getting discouraged, but I had one resource left that had been of good service in similar emergencies. Firmly but kindly I told him my name was Mark Twain, and I awaited results. There was none. He was not fazed a bit. "Phwere's your order to see Mr. Daly?" he asked. I handed him the note, and he examined it intently.

"My friend," I remarked, "you can read that better if you hold it the other side up."

But he took no notice of the suggestion, and finally asked: "Where's Mr. Daly's name?"

"There it is," I told him, "on the top of the page."

"That's all right," he said, "that's where he always puts it; but I don't see the 'W' in his name," and he eyed me distrustfully. Finally he asked, "Phwat do yez want to see Mr. Daly for?"

"Business."

"Business?"

"Yes." It was my only hope.

"Pwhat kind—theaters?" That was too much.

"No."

"What kind of shows, then?"

"Bench-shows." It was risky, but I was desperate.

"Bench-shows, is it—where?" The big man's face changed, and he began to look interested.

"New Haven."

"New Haven, it is? Ah, that's going to be a fine show. I'm glad to see you. Did you see a big dog in the other room?"

"Yes."

"How much do you think that dog weighs?"

"One hundred and forty-five pounds."

"Look at that, now! He's a good judge of dogs, and no mistake. He weighs all of one hundred and thirty-eight. Sit down and shmoke—go on and shmoke your cigar, I'll tell Mr. Daly you are here."

In a few minutes I was on the stage shaking hands with Mr. Daly, and the big man standing around glowing with satisfaction. "Come around in front," said Mr. Daly, "and see the performance. I will put you into my own box."

And as I moved away I heard my honest friend mutter, "Well, he desarves it."

THE FORGIVING DRUGGIST

Washington, D.C., c. September 1890

Twain spoke at a banquet sponsored by the National Wholesale Druggists Association.

About a thousand years ago, approximately, I was apprenticed, as a printer's devil to learn the trade, in common with three other boys about my own age. There came to the village a long-legged individual of about nineteen, from one of the interior counties; fish-eyed, no expression, and without the suggestion of a smile—couldn't have smiled for a salary. We took him for a fool, and thought we would try and scare him to death.

We went to the village druggist and borrowed a skeleton. The skeleton didn't belong to the druggist, but he had imported it for the village doctor, because the doctor thought he would send away for it, having some delicacy about using—well, the price of the skeleton at that time was fifty dollars. I don't know how high they go now, but probably much higher, on account of the tariff.

We borrowed this skeleton about nine o'clock at night, and we got this man—Nicodemus Dodge was his name—we got him downtown out of the way, and then we put the skeleton into his bed. He lived in a little one-storied log cabin in the middle of a vacant lot. We left him to get home by himself. We enjoyed the result in the light of anticipation; but by-and-by we began to drop into silence; the possible consequences began to prey upon us. Suppose that it frightens him into madness, overturns his reason, and sends him screeching through the streets! We shall spend sleepless nights the rest of our days. Everybody was afraid.

By-and-by it was forced to the lips of one of us that we had better go at once and see what was happening. Loaded down with crime we approached that hut and peeped through the window. That long-legged critter was sitting on his bed, with a hunk of gingerbread in his hand, and between the bites he played a tune on a Jew's harp. There he sat, perfectly happy, and all around him on the bed were toys and jimcracks and striped candy. The darned cuss has gone and sold the skeleton for five dollars. The druggist's fifty-dollar skeleton had gone.

We went in tears to that druggist and explained the matter. We couldn't have raised fifty dollars in two hundred and fifty years. We were getting board and clothing for the first year, clothing and board for the second year, and both of them for the third year. But the druggist forgave us on the spot, but he said he would like us to let him have our skeletons when we were done with them. There couldn't be anything fairer than that; we spouted our skeletons and went away comfortable. But from that time the druggist's prosperity ceased. That was one of the most unfortunate speculations he ever went into.

After some years one of the boys went and got drowned; that was one skeleton gone, and I tell you the druggist felt pretty bad about it. A few years after that another of the boys went up in a balloon. He was to get five dollars an hour for it. When he gets back there will be owing him a billion dollars. The druggist's property was decreasing right along. After a few more years the third boy tried an experiment to see if a dynamite charge would go off. It went all right. They found some of him—perhaps a vest pocket full; still it was enough to show that some more of that estate was gone. The druggist was getting along in years, and he commenced to correspond with me. I have been the best correspondent he has. He is the sweetest natured man I ever saw; always mild and polite, and never wants to hurry me at all. I get a letter from him every now and then, and he never refers to my form as a skeleton; he says:

"Well, how is it getting along—is it in good repair?"

I got a nice message from him recently—said he was getting old and the property was depreciating in value; if I could let him have a part of it now he would give time on the balance. Think of the graceful way in which he does everything—the generosity of it all. You cannot find a finer character than that. It is the gracious characteristic of all druggists.

SOURCE: *The Medical Standard*. Volume 32. No. 1. January 1909. Chicago: G. P. Engelhard and Company.

AN "UNDELIVERED" SPEECH

Philadelphia, March 25, 1895

Howells (or the compiler F. A. Nast) believed Twain did not deliver this speech, as the occasion of it, the launching of the steamship St. Paul, *was postponed. However, a pre-launch lunch was held at which the congratulatory speeches, including Twain's, were indeed made.*

Day after tomorrow I sail for England in a ship of this line, the *Paris*. It will be my fourteenth crossing in three years and a half. Therefore, my presence here, as you see, is quite natural, quite commercial. I am interested in ships. They interest me more now than hotels do. When a new ship is launched I feel a desire to go and see if she will be good quarters for me to live in, particularly if she belongs to this line, for it is by this line that I have done most of my ferrying.

People wonder why I go so much. Well, I go partly for my health, partly to familiarize myself with the road. I have gone over the same road so many times now that I know all the whales that belong along the route, and latterly it is an embarrassment to me to meet them, for they do not look glad to see me, but annoyed, and they seem to say: "Here is this old derelict again."

Earlier in life this would have pained me and made me ashamed, but I am older now, and when I am behaving myself, and doing right, I do not care for a whale's opinion about me. When we are young we generally estimate an opinion by the size of the person that holds it, but later we find that that is an uncertain rule, for we realize that there are times when a hornet's opinion disturbs us more than an emperor's.

I do not mean that I care nothing at all for a whale's opinion, for that would be going to too great a length. Of course, it is better to have the good opinion of a whale than his disapproval; but my position is that if you cannot have a whale's good opinion, except at some sacrifice of principle or personal dignity, it is better to try to live without it. That is my idea about whales.

Yes, I have gone over that same route so often that I know my way without a compass, just by the waves. I know all the large waves and a good many of the small ones. Also the sunsets. I know every sunset and where it belongs just by its color. Necessarily, then, I do not make the passage now for scenery. That is all gone by.

What I prize most is safety, and in the second place swift transit and handiness. These are best furnished by the American line, whose watertight compartments have no passage through them, no doors to be left open, and consequently no way for water to get from one of them to another in time of collision. If you nullify the peril which collisions threaten you with, you nullify the only very serious peril which attends voyages in the great liners of our day, and makes voyaging safer than staying at home.

When the *Paris* was half-torn to pieces some years ago, enough of the Atlantic ebbed and flowed through one end of her, during her long agony, to sink the fleets of the world if distributed among them; but she floated in perfect safety, and no life was lost. In time of collision the rock of Gibraltar is not safer than the *Paris* and other great ships of this line. This seems to be the only great line in the world that takes a passenger from metropolis to metropolis without the intervention of tugs and barges or bridges—takes him through without breaking bulk, so to speak.

On the English side he lands at a dock; on the dock a special train is waiting; in an hour and three-quarters he is in London. Nothing could be handier. If your journey were from a sand-pit on our side to a lighthouse on the other, you could make it quicker by other lines, but that is not the case. The journey is from the city of New York to the city of London, and no line can do that journey quicker than this one, nor anywhere near as conveniently and handily. And when the passenger lands on our side he lands on the American side of the river, not in the provinces. As a very learned man said on the last voyage . . . "When we land a passenger on the American side there's nothing betwixt him and his hotel but hell and the hackman."

I am glad, with you and the nation, to welcome the new ship. She is another pride, another consolation, for a great country whose mighty fleets have all vanished, and which has almost forgotten what it is to fly its flag to sea. I am not sure as to which St. Paul she is named for. Some think it is the one that is on the upper Mississippi, but the head quartermaster told me it was the one that killed Goliath. But it is not important. No matter which it is, let us give her hearty welcome and godspeed.

DIE SCHRECKEN DER DEUTSHEN SPRACHE ("HORRORS OF THE GERMAN LANGUAGE")

Vienna, October 31, 1897

Twain addressed the Vienna Press Club at the Concordia Festneipe. Twain dramatized his comic adventures of learning German most lengthily and comically in A Tramp Abroad. *Here he translates his speech "literally," to highlight his grammatical and rhetorical challenges.*

It has me deeply touched, my gentlemen, here so hospitably received to be. From colleagues out of my own profession, in this from my own home so far distant land. My heart is full of gratitude, but my poverty of German words forces me to greater economy of expression. Excuse you, my gentlemen, that I read off, what I you say will.[16]

The German language speak I not good, but have numerous connoisseurs me assured that I her write like an angel. Maybe—maybe—I know not. Have till now no acquaintance with the angels had. That comes later—when it the dear God please—it has no hurry.

Since long, my gentlemen, have I the passionate longing nursed a speech on German to hold, but one has me not permitted. Men, who no feeling for the art had, laid me ever hindrance in the way and made naught my desire—sometimes by excuses, often by force. Always said these men to me: "Keep you still, your Highness! Silence! For God's sake seek another way and means yourself obnoxious to make."

In the present case, as usual it is me difficult become, for me the permission to obtain. The committee sorrowed deeply, but could me the permission not grant on account of a law which from the Concordia demands she shall the German language protect. *Du liebe Zeit!* How so had one to me this say could—might—dared—should? I am indeed the truest friend of the German language—and not only now, but from long since—yes, before twenty years already. And never have I the desire had the noble language to hurt; to the contrary, only

---

16. According to Twain's friend and the editor of Twain's first collection of speeches, he did not *read* the speech at all; he *performed* it, as he almost always did while public speaking.

wished she to improve—I would her only reform. It is the dream of my life been. I have already visits by the various German governments paid and for contracts prayed. I am now to Austria in the same task come. I would only some changes effect. I would only the language method—the luxurious, elaborate construction compress, the eternal parenthesis suppress, do away with, annihilate; the introduction of more than thirteen subjects in one sentence forbid; the verb so far to the front pull that one it without a telescope discover can. With one word, my gentlemen, I would your beloved language simplify so that, my gentlemen, when you her for prayer need, One her yonder-up understands.

I beseech you, from me yourself counsel to let, execute these mentioned reforms. Then will you an elegant language possess, and afterward, when you some thing say will, will you at least yourself understand what you said had. But often nowadays, when you a mile-long sentence from you given and you yourself somewhat have rested, then must you have a touching inquisitiveness have yourself to determine what you actually spoken have. Before several days has the correspondent of a local paper a sentence constructed which hundred and twelve words contain, and therein were seven parentheses smuggled in, and the subject seven times changed. Think you only, my gentlemen, in the course of the voyage of a single sentence must the poor, persecuted, fatigued subject seven times change position!

Now, when we the mentioned reforms execute, will it no longer so bad be. *Doch noch eins.* I might gladly the separable verb also a little bit reform. I might none do let what Schiller did: he has the whole history of the Thirty Years' War between the two members of a separable verb in-pushed. That has even Germany itself aroused, and one has Schiller the permission refused the History of the Hundred Years' War to compose—God be it thanked! After all these reforms established be will, will the German language the noblest and the prettiest on the world be.

Since to you now, my gentlemen, the character of my mission known is, beseech I you so friendly to be and to me your valuable help grant. Mr. Potzl has the public believed make would that I to Vienna come am in order the bridges to clog up and the traffic to hinder, while I observations gather and note. Allow you yourselves but not from him deceived. My frequent presence on the bridges has an entirely innocent ground. Yonder gives it the necessary space, yonder can one a noble long German sentence elaborate, the bridge-railing along, and his whole contents with one glance overlook. On the one end of the railing pasted I the first member of a separable verb and the final member cleave I to the other end—then spread the body of the sentence between it out! Usually are for my purposes the bridges of the city long enough; when I but Potzl's writings study will I ride out and use the glorious endless imperial bridge. But this is a calumny; Potzl writes the prettiest German. Perhaps not so pliable as the mine, but in many details much better. Excuse you these flatteries. These are well deserved.

Now I my speech execute—no, I would say I bring her to the close. I am a foreigner—but here, under you, have I it entirely forgotten. And so again and yet again proffer I you my heartiest thanks.

TO THE WHITEFRIARS

London, June 16, 1899

The Whitefriars Club, founded in the eighteenth century by Samuel Johnson, gave a dinner for Twain, who had been made an honorary member in 1874. Howells writes: "The toast of 'Our Guest' was proposed by Louis F. Austin, of the Illustrated London News, *and in the course of some humorous remarks [Twain] referred to the vow and to the imaginary woes of the 'Friars,' as the members of the club style themselves."*

Mr. Chairman and Brethren of the Vow—in whatever the vow is; for although I have been a member of this club for five-and-twenty years, I don't know any more about what that vow is than Mr. Austin seems to. But whatever the vow is, I don't care what it is. I have made a thousand vows.

There is no pleasure comparable to making a vow in the presence of one who appreciates that vow, in the presence of men who honor and appreciate you for making the vow, and men who admire you for making the vow.

There is only one pleasure higher than that, and that is to get outside and break the vow. A vow is always a pledge of some kind or other for the protection of your own morals and principles or somebody else's, and generally, by the irony of fate, it is for the protection of your own morals.

Hence we have pledges that make us eschew tobacco or wine, and while you are taking the pledge there is a holy influence about that makes you feel you are reformed, and that you can never be so happy again in this world until—you get outside and take a drink.

I had forgotten that I was a member of this club—it is so long ago. But now I remember that I was here five-and-twenty years ago, and that I was then at a dinner of the Whitefriars Club, and it was in those old days when you had just made two great finds. All London was talking about nothing else than that they had found Livingstone, and

53

that the lost Sir Roger Tichborne had been found—and they were trying him for it.

And at the dinner, Chairman—(I do not know who he was)—failed to come to time. The gentleman who had been appointed to pay me the customary compliments and to introduce me forgot the compliments, and did not know what they were.

And George Augustus Sala came in at the last moment, just when I was about to go without compliments altogether. And that man was a gifted man. They just called on him instantaneously, while he was going to sit down, to introduce the stranger, and Sala made one of those marvelous speeches which he was capable of making. I think no man talked so fast as Sala did. One did not need wine while he was making a speech. The rapidity of his utterance made a man drunk in a minute. An incomparable speech was that, an impromptu speech, and an impromptu speech is a seldom thing, and he did it so well.

He went into the whole history of the United States, and made it entirely new to me. He filled it with episodes and incidents that Washington never heard of, and he did it so convincingly that although I knew none of it had happened, from that day to this I do not know any history but Sala's.

I do not know anything so sad as a dinner where you are going to get up and say something by-and-by, and you do not know what it is. You sit and wonder and wonder what the gentleman is going to say who is going to introduce you. You know that if he says something severe, that if he will deride you, or traduce you, or do anything of that kind, he will furnish you with a text, because anybody can get up and talk against that.

Anybody can get up and straighten out his character. But when a gentleman gets up and merely tells the truth about you, what can you do?

Mr. Austin has done well. He has supplied so many texts that I will have to drop out a lot of them, and that is about as difficult as when you do not have any text at all. Now, he made a beautiful and smooth speech without any difficulty at all, and I could have done that if I had gone on with the schooling with which I began. I see here a gentleman on my left who was my master in the art of oratory more than twenty-five years ago.

When I look upon the inspiring face of Mr. Depew, it carries me a long way back. An old and valued friend of mine is he, and I saw his career as it came along, and it has reached pretty well up to now, when he, by another miscarriage of justice, is a United States Senator. But those were delightful days when I was taking lessons in oratory.

My other master—the Ambassador—is not here yet. Under those two gentlemen I learned to make after-dinner speeches, and it was charming.

You know the New England dinner is the great occasion on the other side of the water. It is held every year to celebrate the landing of the Pilgrims. Those Pilgrims were a lot of people who were not needed in England, and you know they had great rivalry, and they were persuaded to go elsewhere, and they chartered a ship called *Mayflower* and set sail, and I have heard it said that they pumped the Atlantic Ocean through that ship sixteen times.

They fell in over there with the Dutch from Rotterdam, Amsterdam, and a lot of other places with profane names, and it is from that gang that Mr. Depew is descended.

On the other hand, Mr. [Joseph] Choate is descended from those Puritans who landed on a bitter night in December. Every year those people used to meet at a great banquet in New York, and those masters of mind in oratory had to make speeches. It was Doctor Depew's business to get up there and apologize for the Dutch, and Mr. Choate had to get up later and explain the crimes of the Puritans, and grand, beautiful times we used to have.

It is curious that after that long lapse of time I meet the Whitefriars again, some looking as young and fresh as in the old days, others showing a certain amount of wear and tear, and here, after all this time, I find one of the masters of oratory and the others named in the list.

And here we three meet again as exiles on one pretext or another, and you will notice that while we are absent there is a pleasing tranquility in America—a building up of public confidence. We are doing the best we can for our country. I think we have spent our lives in serving our country, and we never serve it to greater advantage than when we get out of it.

But impromptu speaking—that is what I was trying to learn. That is a difficult thing. I used to do it in this way. I used to begin about a week ahead, and write out my impromptu speech and get it by heart. Then I brought it to the New England dinner printed on a piece of paper in my pocket, so that I could pass it to the reporters all cut and dried, and in order to do an impromptu speech as it should be done you have to indicate the places for pauses and hesitations. I put them all in it. And then you want the applause in the right places.

When I got to the place where it should come in, if it did not come in I did not care, but I had it marked in the paper. And these masters of mind used to wonder why it was my speech came out in the morning in the first person, while theirs went through the butchery of synopsis.

I do that kind of speech (I mean an offhand speech), and do it well, and make no mistake in such a way to deceive the audience completely and make that audience believe it is an impromptu speech—that is art.

I was frightened out of it at last by an experience of Doctor Hayes. He was a sort of Nansen of that day. He had been to the North Pole, and it made him celebrated. He had even seen the polar bear climb the pole.

He had made one of those magnificent voyages such as Nansen made, and in those days when a man did anything which greatly distinguished him for the moment he had to come on to the lecture platform and tell all about it.

Doctor Hayes was a great, magnificent creature like Nansen, superbly built. He was to appear in Boston. He wrote his lecture out, and it was his purpose to read it from manuscript; but in an evil hour he concluded that it would be a good thing to preface it with something rather handsome, poetical, and beautiful that he could get off by heart and deliver as if it were the thought of the moment.

He had not had my experience, and could not do that. He came on the platform, held his manuscript down, and began with a beautiful piece of oratory. He spoke something like this: "When a lonely human being, a pigmy in the midst of the architecture of nature, stands solitary on those icy waters and looks abroad to the horizon and sees mighty castles and temples of eternal ice raising up their pinnacles tipped by the pencil of the departing sun—"

Here a man came across the platform and touched him on the shoulder, and said: "One minute." And then to the audience:

"Is Mrs. John Smith in the house? Her husband has slipped on the ice and broken his leg."

And you could see the Mrs. John Smiths get up everywhere and drift out of the house, and it made great gaps everywhere. Then Doctor Hayes began again: "When a lonely man, a pigmy in the architecture—"

The janitor came in again and shouted: "It is not Mrs. John Smith! It is Mrs. John Jones!"

Then all the Mrs. Joneses got up and left. Once more the speaker started, and was in the midst of the sentence when he was interrupted again, and the result was that the lecture was not delivered. But the lecturer interviewed the janitor afterward in a private room, and of the fragments of the janitor they took "twelve basketsful."

Now, I don't want to sit down just in this way. I have been talking with so much levity that I have said no serious thing, and you are really no better or wiser, although Robert Buchanan has suggested that I am a person who deals in wisdom. I have said nothing which would make you better than when you came here.

I should be sorry to sit down without having said one serious word which you can carry home and relate to your children and the old people who are not able to get away.

And this is just a little maxim which has saved me from many a difficulty and many a disaster, and in times of tribulation and uncertainty has come to my rescue, as it shall to yours if you observe it as I do day and night.

I always use it in an emergency, and you can take it home as a legacy from me, and it is: "When in doubt, tell the truth."

THE DAY WE CELEBRATE (I)

London, July 4, 1899

Twain addressed the American Society of London on Independence Day (see also his July 4th speech to the same group in 1907, "The Day We Celebrate (II)"). He touches on the famous mistaken-hat anecdote here that he more fully and humorously elaborates upon in "Books, Authors and Hats" (June 25, 1907).

I noticed in Ambassador Choate's speech that he said: "You may be Americans or Englishmen, but you cannot be both at the same time." You responded by applause.

Consider the effect of a short residence here. I find the Ambassador rises first to speak to a toast, followed by a Senator, and I come third. What a subtle tribute that to monarchial influence of the country when you place rank above respectability!

I was born modest, and if I had not been things like this would force it upon me. I understand it quite well. I am here to see that between them they do justice to the day we celebrate, and in case they do not I must do it myself. But I notice they have considered this day merely from one side—its sentimental, patriotic, poetic side. But it has another side. It has a commercial, a business side that needs reforming. It has a historical side.

I do not say "an" historical side, because I am speaking the American language. I do not see why our cousins should continue to say "an" hospital, "an" historical fact, "an" horse. It seems to me the Congress of Women, now in session, should look to it. I think "an" is having a little too much to do with it. It comes of habit, which accounts for many things.

Yesterday, for example, I was at a luncheon party. At the end of the party a great dignitary of the English Established Church went away half an hour before anybody else and carried off my hat. Now, that was an innocent act on his part. He went out first, and of course had the choice of hats. As a rule I try to get out first myself. But I hold that

58

it was an innocent, unconscious act, due, perhaps, to heredity. He was thinking about ecclesiastical matters, and when a man is in that condition of mind he will take anybody's hat. The result was that the whole afternoon I was under the influence of his clerical hat and could not tell a lie. Of course, he was hard at it.

It is a compliment to both of us. His hat fitted me exactly; my hat fitted him exactly. So I judge I was born to rise to high dignity in the Church some how or other, but I do not know what he was born for. That is an illustration of the influence of habit, and it is perceptible here when they say "an" hospital, "an" European, "an" historical.

The business aspects of the Fourth of July is not perfect as it stands. See what it costs us every year with loss of life, the crippling of thousands with its fireworks, and the burning down of property. It is not only sacred to patriotism and universal freedom, but to the surgeon, the undertaker, the insurance offices—and they are working it for all it is worth.

I am pleased to see that we have a cessation of war for the time. This coming from me, a soldier, you will appreciate. I was a soldier in the Southern war for two weeks, and when gentlemen get up to speak of the great deeds our army and navy have recently done, why, it goes all through me and fires up the old war spirit. I had in my first engagement three horses shot under me. The next ones went over my head, the next hit me in the back. Then I retired to meet an engagement.

I thank you, gentlemen, for making even a slight reference to the war profession, in which I distinguished myself, short as my career was.

LITERATURE

London, May 2, 1900

Twain responded to the toast "Literature" at the Royal Literary Fund banquet at the Hotel Cecil.

Mr. Hope has been able to deal adequately with this toast without assistance from me. Still, I was born generous. If he had advanced any theories that needed refutation or correction I would have attended to them, and if he had made any statements stronger than those which he is in the habit of making I would have dealt with them.

In fact, I was surprised at the mildness of his statements. I could not have made such statements if I had preferred to, because to exaggerate is the only way I can approximate to the truth. You cannot have a theory without principles. Principles is another name for prejudices. I have no prejudices in politics, religion, literature, or anything else.

I am now on my way to my own country to run for the presidency because there are not yet enough candidates in the field, and those who have entered are too much hampered by their own principles, which are prejudices.

I propose to go there to purify the political atmosphere. I am in favor of everything everybody is in favor of. What you should do is to satisfy the whole nation, not half of it, for then you would only be half a President.

There could not be a broader platform than mine. I am in favor of anything and everything—of temperance and intemperance, morality and qualified immorality, gold standard and free silver.

I have tried all sorts of things, and that is why I want to try the great position of ruler of a country. I have been in turn reporter, editor, publisher, author, lawyer, burglar. I have worked my way up, and wish to continue to do so.

I read today in a magazine article that Christendom issued last year fifty-five thousand new books. Consider what that means! Fifty-five thousand new books meant fifty-four thousand new authors. We are going to have them all on our hands to take care of sooner or later. Therefore, double your subscriptions to the literary fund!

HENRY IRVING

London, June 9, 1900

Twain gave a toast to "The Drama" at the Dramatic and Literary Society of London's welcome-home dinner at the Savoy Hotel for Sir Henry Irving, who had been on tour in America.

I find my task a very easy one. I have been a dramatist for thirty years. I have had an ambition in all that time to overdo the work of the Spaniard who said he left behind him four hundred dramas when he died. I leave behind me four hundred and fifteen, and am not yet dead.

The greatest of all the arts is to write a drama. It is a most difficult thing. It requires the highest talent possible and the rarest gifts. No, there is another talent that ranks with it—for anybody can write a drama—I had four hundred of them—but to get one accepted requires real ability. And I have never had that felicity yet.

But human nature is so constructed, we are so persistent, that when we know that we are born to a thing we do not care what the world thinks about it. We go on exploiting that talent year after year, as I have done. I shall go on writing dramas, and some day the impossible may happen, but I am not looking for it.

In writing plays the chief thing is novelty. The world grows tired of solid forms in all the arts. I struck a new idea myself years ago. I was not surprised at it. I was always expecting it would happen. A person who has suffered disappointment for many years loses confidence, and I thought I had better make inquiries before I exploited my new idea of doing a drama in the form of a dream, so I wrote to a great authority on knowledge of all kinds, and asked him whether it was new.

I could depend upon him. He lived in my dear home in America—that dear home, dearer to me through taxes. He sent me a list of plays in which that old device had been used, and he said that there was also a modern lot. He traveled back to China and to a play dated two thousand six hundred years before the Christian era. He said he would follow it up with a list of the previous plays of the kind, and in his innocence would have carried them back to the Flood.

That is the most discouraging thing that has ever happened to me in my dramatic career. I have done a world of good in a silent and private way, and have furnished Sir Henry Irving with plays and plays and plays. What has he achieved through that influence? See where he stands now—on the summit of his art in two worlds—and it was I who put him there—that partly put him there.

I need not enlarge upon the influence the drama has exerted upon civilization. It has made good morals entertaining. I am to be followed by Mr. Pinero. I conceive that we stand at the head of the profession. He has not written as many plays as I have, but he has had that God-given talent, which I lack, of working them off on the manager. I couple his name with this toast, and add the hope that his influence will be supported in exercising his masterly handicraft in that great gift, and that he will long live to continue his fine work.

GALVESTON ORPHAN BAZAAR

New York City, October 17, 1900

In September 8, 1900, a hurricane devastated Galveston, Texas, killing several thousand people. Twain spoke at a fundraiser at the Waldorf-Astoria in aid of the orphans.

I expected that the Governor of Texas would occupy this place first and would speak to you, and in the course of his remarks would drop a text for me to talk from; but with the proverbial obstinacy that is proverbial with governors, they go back on their duties, and he has not come here, and has not furnished me with a text, and I am here without a text. I have no text except what you furnish me with your handsome faces, and—but I won't continue that, for I could go on forever about attractive faces, beautiful dresses, and other things. But, after all, compliments should be in order in a place like this.

I have been in New York two or three days, and have been in a condition of strict diligence night and day, the object of this diligence being to regulate the moral and political situation on this planet—put it on a sound basis—and when you are regulating the conditions of a planet it requires a great deal of talk in a great many kinds of ways, and when you have talked a lot the emptier you get, and get also in a position of corking. When I am situated like that, with nothing to say, I feel as though I were a sort of fraud; I seem to be playing a part, and please consider I am playing a part for want of something better, and this is not unfamiliar to me; I have often done this before.

When I was here about eight years ago I was coming up in a car of the elevated road. Very few people were in that car, and on one end of it there was no one, except on the opposite seat, where sat a man about fifty years old, with a most winning face and an elegant eye—a beautiful eye; and I took him from his dress to be a master mechanic, a man who had a vocation. He had with him a very fine little child of about four or five years. I was watching the affection which existed between those two. I judged he was the grandfather, perhaps. It was

64

really a pretty child, and I was admiring her, and as soon as he saw I was admiring her he began to notice me.

I could see his admiration of me in his eye, and I did what everybody else would do—admired the child four times as much, knowing I would get four times as much of his admiration. Things went on very pleasantly. I was making my way into his heart.

By-and-by, when he almost reached the station where he was to get off, he got up, crossed over, and he said: "Now I am going to say something to you which I hope you will regard as a compliment." And then he went on to say: "I have never seen Mark Twain, but I have seen a portrait of him, and any friend of mine will tell you that when I have once seen a portrait of a man I place it in my eye and store it away in my memory, and I can tell you now that you look enough like Mark Twain to be his brother. Now," he said, "I hope you take this as a compliment. Yes, you are a very good imitation; but when I come to look closer, you are probably not that man."

I said: "I will be frank with you. In my desire to look like that excellent character I have dressed for the character; I have been playing a part."

He said: "That is all right, that is all right; you look very well on the outside, but when it comes to the inside you are not in it with the original."

So when I come to a place like this with nothing valuable to say I always play a part. But I will say before I sit down that when it comes to saying anything here I will express myself in this way: I am heartily in sympathy with you in your efforts to help those who were sufferers in this calamity, and in your desire to help those who were rendered homeless, and in saying this I wish to impress on you the fact that I am not playing a part.

SOCIETY OF AMERICAN AUTHORS

New York City, November 15, 1900

Just before his 65th birthday, the Society of American Authors hosted a reception in his honor at Delmonico's Restaurant. Twain was accompanied by his wife and daughter. After the society chairman Rastus Ransom's introduction, Twain spoke.

Chairman, Ladies and Gentlemen,

It seems a most difficult thing for any man to say anything about me that is not complimentary. I don't know what the charm is about me which makes it impossible for a person to say a harsh thing about me and say it heartily, as if he was glad to say it.

If this thing keeps on it will make me believe that I am what these kind chairmen say of me. In introducing me, Judge Ransom spoke of my modesty as if he was envious of me. I would like to have one man come out flat-footed and say something harsh and disparaging of me, even if it were true. I thought at one time, as the learned judge was speaking, that I had found that man; but he wound up, like all the others, by saying complimentary things.

I am constructed like everybody else, and enjoy a compliment as well as any other fool, but I do like to have the other side presented. And there is another side. I have a wicked side. Estimable friends who know all about it would tell you and take a certain delight in telling you things that I have done, and things further that I have not repented.

The real life that I live, and the real life that I suppose all of you live, is a life of interior sin. That is what makes life valuable and pleasant. To lead a life of undiscovered sin! That is true joy.

Judge Ransom seems to have all the virtues that he ascribes to me. But, oh my! if you could throw an X-ray through him. We are a pair. I have made a life-study of trying to appear to be what he seems to think I am. Everybody believes that I am a monument of all the virtues, but it is nothing of the sort. I am living two lives, and it keeps me pretty busy.

Some day there will be a chairman who will forget some of these merits of mine, and then he will make a speech.

I have more personal vanity than modesty, and twice as much veracity as the two put together.

When that fearless and forgetful chairman is found there will be another story told. At the Press Club recently I thought that I had found him. He started in in the way that I knew I should be painted with all sincerity, and was leading to things that would not be to my credit; but when he said that he never read a book of mine I knew at once that he was a liar, because he never could have had all the wit and intelligence with which he was blessed unless he had read my works as a basis.

I like compliments. I like to go home and tell them all over again to the members of my family. They don't believe them, but I like to tell them in the home circle, all the same. I like to dream of them if I can.

I thank everybody for their compliments, but I don't think that I am praised any more than I am entitled to be.

DISAPPEARANCE OF LITERATURE

New York City, November 20, 1900

Mr. Clemens addressed the Nineteenth Century Club at Sherry's restaurant and responded to the toast "The Disappearance of Literature." The chairman of the club, Elgin Gould, introduced Twain, teasing Twain for the language offenses Twain had made in Germany. See also "Horrors of the German Language" (October 31, 1897) and a later variation on his Darwin anecdote in "Books, Authors, and Hats" (June 25, 1907).

It wasn't necessary for your chairman to apologize for me in Germany. It wasn't necessary at all. Instead of that he ought to have impressed upon those poor benighted Teutons the service I rendered them. Their language had needed untangling for a good many years. Nobody else seemed to want to take the job, and so I took it, and I flatter myself that I made a pretty good job of it. The Germans have an inhuman way of cutting up their verbs. Now a verb has a hard time enough of it in this world when it's all together. It's downright inhuman to split it up. But that's just what those Germans do. They take part of a verb and put it down here, like a stake, and they take the other part of it and put it away over yonder like another stake, and between these two limits they just shovel in German. I maintain that there is no necessity for apologizing for a man who helped in a small way to stop such mutilation.

We have heard a discussion tonight on the disappearance of literature. That's no new thing. That's what certain kinds of literature have been doing for several years. The fact is, my friends, that the fashion in literature changes, and the literary tailors have to change their cuts or go out of business. Professor Winchester here, if I remember fairly correctly what he said, remarked that few, if any, of the novels produced today would live as long as the novels of Walter Scott. That may be his notion. Maybe he is right; but so far as I am concerned, I don't care if they don't.

Professor Winchester also said something about there being no modern epics like *Paradise Lost*. I guess he's right. He talked as if he

68

was pretty familiar with that piece of literary work, and nobody would suppose that he never had read it. I don't believe any of you have ever read *Paradise Lost*, and you don't want to. That's something that you just want to take on trust. It's a classic, just as Professor Winchester says, and it meets his definition of a classic—something that everybody wants to have read and nobody wants to read.

Professor Trent also had a good deal to say about the disappearance of literature. He said that Scott would outlive all his critics. I guess that's true. The fact of the business is, you've got to be one of two ages to appreciate Scott. When you're eighteen you can read *Ivanhoe*, and you want to wait until you are ninety to read some of the rest. It takes a pretty well-regulated, abstemious critic to live ninety years.

But as much as these two gentlemen have talked about the disappearance of literature, they didn't say anything about my books. Maybe they think they've disappeared. If they do, that just shows their ignorance on the general subject of literature. I am not as young as I was several years ago, and maybe I'm not so fashionable, but I'd be willing to take my chances with Mr. Scott tomorrow morning in selling a piece of literature to the Century Publishing Company. And I haven't got much of a pull here, either. I often think that the highest compliment ever paid to my poor efforts was paid by Darwin through President Eliot, of Harvard College. At least, Eliot said it was a compliment, and I always take the opinion of great men like college presidents on all such subjects as that.

I went out to Cambridge one day a few years ago and called on President Eliot. In the course of the conversation he said that he had just returned from England, and that he was very much touched by what he considered the high compliment Darwin was paying to my books, and he went on to tell me something like this:

"Do you know that there is one room in Darwin's house, his bedroom, where the housemaid is never allowed to touch two things? One is a plant he is growing and studying while it grows" (it was one of those insect-devouring plants which consumed bugs and beetles and things for the particular delectation of Mr. Darwin) "and the other some books that lie on the night table at the head of his bed. They are your books, Mr. Clemens, and Mr. Darwin reads them every night to lull him to sleep."

My friends, I thoroughly appreciated that compliment, and considered it the highest one that was ever paid to me. To be the means of soothing to sleep a brain teeming with bugs and squirming things like Darwin's was something that I had never hoped for, and now that he is dead I never hope to be able to do it again.

MUNICIPAL GOVERNMENT

New York City, December 6, 1900

Twain addressed the 66th annual dinner of the St. Nicholas Society at Delmonico's Restaurant. During the toasts, Donald Sage Mackay, minister of the Collegiate Church of Saint Nicholas, described the author's good work: "Mark Twain is as true a preacher of true righteousness as any bishop, priest, or minister of any church today, because he moves men to forget their faults by cheerful well-doing instead of making them sour and morbid by everlastingly bending their attention to the seamy and sober side of life."

Mr. Chairman and Gentlemen of the St. Nicholas Society,

These are, indeed, prosperous days for me. Night before last, in a speech, the Bishop of the Diocese of New York complimented me for my contribution to theology, and tonight the Reverend Doctor Mackay has elected me to the ministry. I thanked Bishop Potter then for his compliment, and I thank Doctor Mackay now for that promotion. I think that both have discerned in me what I long ago discerned, but what I was afraid the world would never learn to recognize.

In this absence of nine years I find a great improvement in the city of New York. I am glad to speak on that as a toast—"The City of New York." Some say it has improved because I have been away. Others, and I agree with them, say it has improved because I have come back. We must judge of a city, as of a man, by its external appearances and by its inward character. In externals the foreigner coming to these shores is more impressed at first by our skyscrapers. They are new to him. He has not done anything of the sort since he built the tower of Babel. The foreigner is shocked by them.

In the daylight they are ugly. They are—well, too chimneyfied and too snaggy—like a mouth that needs attention from a dentist; like a cemetery that is all monuments and no gravestones. But at night, seen from the river where they are columns towering against the sky, all sparkling with light, they are fairylike; they are beauty more satisfactory to the soul and more enchanting than anything that man has dreamed of since the Arabian nights. We can't always have the beautiful aspect of things. Let us make the most of our sights that are beautiful and let the others go. When your foreigner makes disagreeable comments on New York by daylight, float him down the river at night.

What has made these skyscrapers possible is the elevator. The cigar-box which the European calls a "lift" needs but to be compared with our elevators to be appreciated. The lift stops to reflect between floors. That is all right in a hearse, but not in elevators. The American elevator acts like the man's patent purge—it worked. As the inventor said, "This purge doesn't waste any time fooling around; it attends strictly to business."

That New Yorkers have the cleanest, quickest, and most admirable system of street railways in the world has been forced upon you by the abnormal appreciation you have of your hackman. We ought always to be grateful to him for that service. Nobody else would have brought such a system into existence for us. We ought to build him a monument. We owe him one as much as we owe one to anybody. Let it be a tall one. Nothing permanent, of course; build it of plaster, say. Then gaze at it and realize how grateful we are—for the time being—and then pull it down and throw it on the ash-heap. That's the way to honor your public heroes.

As to our streets, I find them cleaner than they used to be. I miss those dear old landmarks, the symmetrical mountain ranges of dust and dirt that used to be piled up along the streets for the wind and rain to tear down at their pleasure. Yes, New York is cleaner than Bombay. I realize that I have been in Bombay, that I now am in New York; that it is not my duty to flatter Bombay, but rather to flatter New York.

Compared with the wretched attempts of London to light that city, New York may fairly be said to be a well-lighted city. Why, London's attempt at good lighting is almost as bad as London's attempt at rapid transit. There is just one good system of rapid transit in London—the "Tube," and that, of course, had been put in by Americans. Perhaps, after a while, those Americans will come back and give New York also a good underground system. Perhaps they have already begun. I have been so busy since I came back that I haven't had time as yet to go down cellar.

But it is by the laws of the city, it is by the manners of the city, it is by the ideals of the city, it is by the customs of the city and by the municipal government which all these elements correct, support, and foster, by which the foreigner judges the city. It is by these that he realizes that New York may, indeed, hold her head high among the cities of the world. It is by these standards that he knows whether to class the city higher or lower than the other municipalities of the world.

Gentlemen, you have the best municipal government in the world— the purest and the most fragrant. The very angels envy you, and wish they could establish a government like it in heaven. You got it by a noble fidelity to civic duty. You got it by stern and ever-watchful exertion of the great powers with which you are charged by the rights which were handed down to you by your forefathers, by your manly refusal to let base men invade the high places of your government, and by instant retaliation when any public officer has insulted you in the city's name by swerving in the slightest from the upright and full performance of his duty. It is you who have made this city the envy of the cities of the world. God will bless you for it—God will bless you for it. Why, when you approach the final resting-place the angels of heaven will gather at the gates and cry out:

"Here they come! Show them to the archangel's box, and turn the lime-light on them!"

VOTES FOR WOMEN

New York City, January 20, 1901

Twain spoke at the annual meeting of the Hebrew Technical School for Girls at the Temple Emanu-El on Henry Street. The president of the school, Nathaniel Meyers, having asked the audience for contributions, introduced Twain: "In one of Mr. Clemens's works he expressed his opinion of men, saying he had no choice between Hebrew and Gentile, black men or white; to him all men were alike. But I never could find that he expressed his opinion of women; perhaps that opinion was so exalted that he could not express it. We shall now be called to hear what he thinks of women."

Ladies and gentlemen, it is a small help that I can afford, but it is just such help that one can give as coming from the heart through the mouth. The report of Mr. Meyers was admirable, and I was as interested in it as you have been. Why, I'm twice as old as he, and I've had so much experience that I would say to him, when he makes his appeal for help: "Don't make it for today or tomorrow, but collect the money on the spot."

We are all creatures of sudden impulse. We must be worked up by steam, as it were. Get them to write their wills now, or it may be too late by-and-by. Fifteen or twenty years ago I had an experience I shall never forget. I got into a church which was crowded by a sweltering and panting multitude. The city missionary of our town—Hartford—made a telling appeal for help. He told of personal experiences among the poor in cellars and top lofts requiring instances of devotion and help. The poor are always good to the poor. When a person with his millions gives a hundred thousand dollars it makes a great noise in the world, but he does not miss it; it's the widow's mite that makes no noise but does the best work.

I remember on that occasion in the Hartford church the collection was being taken up. The appeal had so stirred me that I could hardly wait for the hat or plate to come my way. I had four hundred dollars in my pocket, and I was anxious to drop it in the plate and wanted to

73

borrow more. But the plate was so long in coming my way that the fever-heat of beneficence was going down lower and lower—going down at the rate of a hundred dollars a minute. The plate was passed too late. When it finally came to me, my enthusiasm had gone down so much that I kept my four hundred dollars—and stole a dime from the plate. So, you see, time sometimes leads to crime.

Oh, many a time have I thought of that and regretted it, and I adjure you all to give while the fever is on you.

Referring to woman's sphere in life, I'll say that woman is always right. For twenty-five years I've been a woman's rights man. I have always believed, long before my mother died, that, with her gray hairs and admirable intellect, perhaps she knew as much as I did. Perhaps she knew as much about voting as I.

I should like to see the time come when women shall help to make the laws. I should like to see that whip-lash, the ballot, in the hands of women. As for this city's government, I don't want to say much, except that it is a shame—a shame; but if I should live twenty-five years longer—and there is no reason why I shouldn't—I think I'll see women handle the ballot. If women had the ballot today, the state of things in this town would not exist.

If all the women in this town had a vote today they would elect a mayor at the next election, and they would rise in their might and change the awful state of things now existing here.

REBELS

New York City, February 11, 1901

Twain spoke at Carnegie Hall to help raise money for the Lincoln Memorial University in Tennessee. February 12, 1901, would have been Abraham Lincoln's 92nd birthday.

Ladies and Gentlemen,

The remainder of my duties as presiding chairman here this evening are but two—only two. One of them is easy, and the other difficult. That is to say, I must introduce the orator, and then keep still and give him a chance. The name of Henry Watterson carries with it its own explanation. It is like an electric light on top of Madison Square Garden; you touch the button and the light flashes up out of the darkness. You mention the name of Henry Watterson, and your minds are at once illuminated with the splendid radiance of his fame and achievements. A journalist, a soldier, an orator, a statesman, a rebel. Yes, he was a rebel; and, better still, now he is a reconstructed rebel.

It is a curious circumstance, a circumstance brought about without any collusion or prearrangement, that he and I, both of whom were rebels related by blood to each other, should be brought here together this evening bearing a tribute in our hands and bowing our heads in reverence to that noble soul who for three years we tried to destroy. I don't know as the fact has ever been mentioned before, but it is a fact, nevertheless. Colonel Watterson and I were both rebels, and we are blood relations. I was a second lieutenant in a Confederate company— for a while—oh, I could have stayed on if I had wanted to. I made myself felt, I left tracks all around the country. I could have stayed on, but it was such weather. I never saw such weather to be out-of-doors in, in all my life.

The Colonel commanded a regiment, and did his part, I suppose, to destroy the Union. He did not succeed, yet if he had obeyed me he would have done so. I had a plan, and I fully intended to drive General Grant into the Pacific Ocean—if I could get transportation. I

75

told Colonel Watterson about it. I told him what he had to do. What I wanted him to do was to surround the Eastern army and wait until I came up. But he was insubordinate; he stuck on some quibble of military etiquette about a second lieutenant giving orders to a colonel or something like that. And what was the consequence? The Union was preserved. This is the first time I believe that that secret has ever been revealed.

No one outside of the family circle, I think, knew it before; but there the facts are. Watterson saved the Union; yes, he saved the Union. And yet there he sits, and not a step has been taken or a movement made toward granting him a pension. That is the way things are done. It is a case where some blushing ought to be done. You ought to blush, and I ought to blush, and he—well, he's a little out of practice now.

TRAINING THAT PAYS

New York City, March 16, 1901

At the monthly meeting of New York City's Male Teachers Association at the Hotel Albert, Twain responded to the state superintendent Charles Skinner's discourse on "Patriotism for the Young."

We cannot all agree. That is most fortunate. If we could all agree, life would be too dull. I believe if we did all agree I would take my departure before my appointed time, that is if I had the courage to do so. I do agree in part with what Mr. Skinner has said. In fact, more than I usually agree with other people. I believe that there are no private citizens in a republic. Every man is an official: above all, he is a policeman. He does not need to wear a helmet and brass buttons, but his duty is to look after the enforcement of the laws.

If patriotism had been taught in the schools years ago, the country would not be in the position it is in today. Mr. Skinner is better satisfied with the present conditions than I am. I would teach patriotism in the schools, and teach it this way: I would throw out the old maxim, "My country, right or wrong," and instead I would say, "My country when she is right."

I would not take my patriotism from my neighbor or from Congress. I should teach the children in the schools that all men are created free and equal. Another that the proper government is that which exists by the consent of the governed. If Mr. Skinner and I had to take care of the public schools I would raise up a lot of patriots who would get into trouble with him.

I should also teach the rising patriot that if he ever became the government of the United States and made a promise that he should keep it. I will not go any further into politics as I would get excited, and I don't like to get excited. I prefer to remain calm. I have been a teacher all my life, and never got a cent for it. . . .

I have a benevolent faculty. It does not always show, but it is there. We have had some millionaires who gave money to colleges. Now we have Mr. [Andrew] Carnegie building sixty-five new libraries. There is an educator for you on a large scale. I was going to do it myself, but when I found out it would cost over five millions I changed my mind, as I was afraid it would bankrupt me.

When I found out Mr. Carnegie was going to do it, I told him he could have my ideas gratis. I said to him, "Are the books that are going to be put into the new libraries on a high moral plane?" If they are not, I told him he had better build the libraries and I would write the books. With the wealth I would get out of writing the books, I could build libraries and then he could write the books.

I am glad that Mr. Carnegie has done this magnificent thing, and as the newspapers have suggested, I hope that other rich men will follow his example and continue to do so until it becomes a habit they cannot break.

SOURCE: *The New York Times*. March 17, 1901.

POETS AS POLICEMEN

New York City, March 23, 1901

Twain spoke at a Lotos Club dinner for New York Governor Benjamin Odell, Jr.

Let us abolish policemen who carry clubs and revolvers, and put in a squad of poets armed to the teeth with poems on Spring and Love. I would be very glad to serve as commissioner, not because I think I am especially qualified, but because I am too tired to work and would like to take a rest.

[William Dean] Howells would go well as my deputy. He is tired too, and needs a rest badly.

I would start in at once to elevate, purify, and depopulate the red-light district. I would assign the most soulful poets to that district, all heavily armed with their poems. Take Chauncey Depew as a sample. I would station them on the corners after they had rounded up all the depraved people of the district so they could not escape, and then have them read from their poems to the poor unfortunates. The plan would be very effective in causing an emigration of the depraved element.

BUSINESS

New York City, March 30, 1901

The Eastman Club, members of which were alumni from Poughkeepsie's East-man College, gave their annual banquet at the Y.M.C.A. Hall on Twenty-third Street. After the banker James G. Cannon's speech, Twain was introduced as a personal friend of Tom Sawyer.

Mr. Cannon has furnished me with texts enough to last as slow a speaker as myself all the rest of the night. I took exception to the introducing of Mr. Cannon as a great financier, as if he were the only great financier present. I am a financier. But my methods are not the same as Mr. Cannon's.

I cannot say that I have turned out the great business man that I thought I was when I began life. But I am comparatively young yet, and may learn. I am rather inclined to believe that what troubled me was that I got the big-head early in the game. I want to explain to you a few points of difference between the principles of business as I see them and those that Mr. Cannon believes in.

He says that the primary rule of business success is loyalty to your employer. That's all right—as a theory. What is the matter with loyalty to yourself? As nearly as I can understand Mr. Cannon's methods, there is one great drawback to them. He wants you to work a great deal. Diligence is a good thing, but taking things easy is much more—restful. My idea is that the employer should be the busy man, and the employee the idle one. The employer should be the worried man, and the employee the happy one. And why not? He gets the salary. My plan is to get another man to do the work for me. In that there's more repose. What I want is repose first, last, and all the time.

Mr. Cannon says that there are three cardinal rules of business success; they are diligence, honesty, and truthfulness. Well, diligence is all right. Let it go as a theory. Honesty is the best policy—when there is money in it. But truthfulness is one of the most dangerous—why, this man is misleading you.

I had an experience today with my wife which illustrates this. I was acknowledging a belated invitation to another dinner for this evening, which seemed to have been sent about ten days ago. It only reached me this morning. I was mortified at the discourtesy into which I had been brought by this delay, and wondered what was being thought of me by my hosts. As I had accepted your invitation, of course I had to send regrets to my other friends.

When I started to write this note my wife came up and stood looking over my shoulder. Women always want to know what is going on. Said she: "Should not that read in the third person?" I conceded that it should, put aside what I was writing, and commenced over again. That seemed to satisfy her, and so she sat down and let me proceed. I then finished my first note—and so sent what I intended. I never could have done this if I had let my wife know the truth about it.

Here is what I wrote:

To the Ohio Society,

I have at this moment received a most kind invitation (eleven days old) from Mr. Southard, president; and a like one (ten days old) from Mr. Bryant, president of the Press Club. I thank the society cordially for the compliment of these invitations, although I am booked elsewhere and cannot come.

But, oh, I should like to know the name of the Lightning Express by which they were forwarded; for I owe a friend a dozen chickens, and I believe it will be cheaper to send eggs instead, and let them develop on the road.

Sincerely yours,
Mark Twain

I want to tell you of some of my experiences in business, and then I will be in a position to lay down one general rule for the guidance of those who want to succeed in business. My first effort was about twenty-five years ago. I took hold of an invention—I don't know now what it was all about, but someone came to me and told me it was a good thing, and that there was lots of money in it. He persuaded me to invest $15,000, and I lived up to my beliefs by engaging a man to develop it. To make a long story short, I sunk $40,000 in it.

Then I took up the publication of a book. I called in a publisher and said to him: "I want you to publish this book along lines which I shall lay down. I am the employer, and you are the employee. I am going to show them some new kinks in the publishing business. And I want you to draw on me for money as you go along," which he did. He drew on me for $56,000. Then I asked him to take the book and call it off. But he refused to do that.

My next venture was with a machine for doing something or other. I knew less about that than I did about the invention. But I sunk $170,000 in the business, and I can't for the life of me recollect what it was the machine was to do.

I was still undismayed. You see, one of the strong points about my business life was that I never gave up. I undertook to publish General Grant's book, and made $140,000 in six months. My axiom is, to succeed in business: avoid my example.

DINNER TO HAMILTON W. MABIE

New York City, April 29, 1901

Mabie was the editor of The Outlook Magazine. *The author Henry Van Dyke introduced Twain, saying: "The longer the speaking goes on tonight the more I wonder how I got this job, and the only explanation I can give for it is that it is the same kind of compensation for the number of articles I have sent to* The Outlook, *to be rejected by Hamilton W. Mabie. There is one man here tonight that has a job cut out for him that none of you would have had—a man whose humor has put a girdle of light around the globe, and whose sense of humor has been an example for all five continents. He is going to speak to you. Gentlemen, you know him best as Mark Twain."*

Mr. Chairman and Gentlemen,

This man knows now how it feels to be the chief guest, and if he has enjoyed it he is the first man I have ever seen in that position that did enjoy it. And I know, by side-remarks which he made to me before his ordeal came upon him, that he was feeling as some of the rest of us have felt under the same circumstances. He was afraid that he would not do himself justice; but he did—to my surprise. It is a most serious thing to be a chief guest on an occasion like this, and it is admirable, it is fine. It is a great compliment to a man that he shall come out of it so gloriously as Mr. Mabie came out of it tonight—to my surprise. He did it well.

He appears to be editor of *The Outlook*, and notwithstanding that, I have every admiration, because when everything is said concerning *The Outlook*, after all one must admit that it is frank in its delinquencies, that it is outspoken in its departures from fact, that it is vigorous in its mistaken criticisms of men like me. I have lived in this world a long, long time, and I know you must not judge a man by the editorials that he puts in his paper. A man is always better than his printed opinions. A man always reserves to himself on the inside a purity and an honesty and a justice that are a credit to him, whereas the things that he prints are just the reverse.

Oh yes, you must not judge a man by what he writes in his paper. Even in an ordinary secular paper a man must observe some care about it; he must be better than the principles which he puts in print. And that is the case with Mr. Mabie. Why, to see what he writes about me and the missionaries you would think he did not have any principles. But that is Mr. Mabie in his public capacity. Mr. Mabie in his private capacity is just as clean a man as I am.

In this very room, a month or two ago, some people admired that portrait; some admired this, but the great majority fastened on that, and said, "There is a portrait that is a beautiful piece of art." When that portrait is a hundred years old it will suggest what were the manners and customs in our time. Just as they talk about Mr. Mabie tonight, in that enthusiastic way, pointing out the various virtues of the man and the grace of his spirit, and all that, so was that portrait talked about. They were enthusiastic, just as we men have been over the character and the work of Mr. Mabie. And when they were through they said that portrait, fine as it is, that work, beautiful as it is, that piece of humanity on that canvas, gracious and fine as it is, does not rise to those perfections that exist in the man himself. Come up, Mr. Alexander. *[The reference was to James W. Alexander, who happened to be sitting beneath the portrait of himself on the wall.]*

Now, I should come up and show myself. But he cannot do it, he cannot do it. He was born that way, he was reared in that way. Let his modesty be an example, and I wish some of you had it, too. But that is just what I have been saying-that portrait, fine as it is, is not as fine as the man it represents, and all the things that have been said about Mr. Mabie, and certainly they have been very nobly worded and beautiful, still fall short of the real Mabie.

SONS OF SCOTLAND FEAST
AND MAKE MERRY

New York City, November 30, 1901

*Twain spoke at the 145th Annual Dinner of the St. Andrew's Society at Del-
monico's Restaurant. The steel magnate Andrew Carnegie, "the Lord Rector
of Dublin," presided.*

The President of St. Andrews, the Lord Rector of Dublin, no, Glasgow,
isn't it? No. Well, he is higher up than I thought he was—told me that
Scotch humor is non-existent. How is he a Lord Rector, anyway?
What does he know about ecclesiastics? I suppose he don't care so long
as the salary is satisfactory.

I have never examined the subject of humor until now. I am surprised to find out how much ground it covers. I have got its divisions
and frontiers down on a piece of paper. I find it defined as a production
of the brain, as the power of the brain to produce something humorous, and the capacity of perceiving humor. The third subdivision is
possessed by all English-speaking people, even the Scotch. Even the
Lord Rector is humorous. He has offered of his own motion to send
me a fine lot of whiskey. That is certainly humor. Goldsmith said the
had found some of the Scotch possessed wit, which is next door to
humor. He didn't overurge the compliment.

Josh Billings defined the difference between humor and wit as that
between the lightning bug and the lightning. There is a conscious
and unconscious humor. That whiskey offer of the Lord Rector's was
one of unconscious humor. A peculiarity of that sort is a man is apt
to forget it.

I have here a few anecdotes to illustrate these definitions. I hope you
will recognize them. I like anecdotes which have had the benefit of
experience and travel, those which have stood the test of time, those
which have laid claim to immortality. Here is one passed around a year
ago, and twelve years old in its Scotch form.

A man receives a telegram telling him that his mother-in-law is dead
and asking, "Shall we embalm, bury or cremate her?" He wired back,

"If these fail, try dissection." Now, the unconscious humor of this was that he thought they'd try all of the three means suggested, anyway.

An old Scotch woman wrote to a friend, "First the child died, then the callant"—for the benefit of those not Scotchmen here, I will say that a callant is a kind of shepherd dog. That is, this is the definition of the Lord Rector, who spends six months in his native land every year to preserve his knowledge of its tongue.

Another instance of unconscious humor was of the Sunday school boy who defined a lie as "An abomination before the Lord and an ever present help in time of trouble." That may have been unconscious humor, but it looked more like hard, cold experience and knowledge of facts.

Then you have the story of the two fashionable ladies talking before a sturdy old Irish washerwoman. One said to the other, "Where did you spend the summer?" "Oh, at Long Branch," was the reply. "But the Irish there; oh, the Irish! Where were you?" she asked her companion in turn. "At Saratoga; but the Irish there, oh, the Irish!" Then spoke up the old Irish woman, and asked, "Why didn't you go to Hades? You wouldn't have found any Irish there."

Let me tell you now of a case of conscious humor. It was of William Cary, late of the *Century*, who died a few weeks ago, a man of the finest spirit and thought. One day a distinguished American called at the *Century* office. There was a new boy on duty as sentry. He gruffly gave the gentleman a seat and bade him wait. A short time after, Mr. Cary came along and said, "Why, what are you doing here?" After explanations, Mr. Cary brought out three pictures, one of Washington, one of Lincoln, and one of Grant. "Now, young man," he said to the boy, "didn't you know that gentleman? Now, look at these pictures carefully, and if any of these gentlemen call, show them right in."

I am grateful for this double recognition. I find that, like St. Andrew, my birthday comes on the 30th of November. In fact, I was sixty-six years old about thirty-four minutes ago. It was cold weather when I was born. What a chance there was of my catching cold! My friends never explained their carelessness, except on the plea of custom, but what does a child of that age care for custom?

SOURCE: *The New York Times*. December 1, 1901.

SIXTY-SEVENTH BIRTHDAY

New York, November 28, 1902

George Harvey, president of the publishing company Harper and Brothers, gave a dinner in Twain's honor at the Metropolitan Club.

I think I ought to be allowed to talk as long as I want to, for the reason that I have cancelled all my winter's engagements of every kind, for good and sufficient reasons, and am making no new engagements for this winter, and, therefore, this is the only chance I shall have to disembowel my skull for a year—close the mouth in that portrait for a year. I want to offer thanks and homage to the chairman for this innovation which he has introduced here, which is an improvement, as I consider it, on the old-fashioned style of conducting occasions like this. That was bad—that was a bad, bad, bad arrangement. Under that old custom the chairman got up and made a speech, he introduced the prisoner at the bar, and covered him all over with compliments, nothing but compliments, not a thing but compliments, never a slur, and sat down and left that man to get up and talk without a text. You cannot talk on compliments; that is not a text. No modest person, and I was born one, can talk on compliments. A man gets up and is filled to the eyes with happy emotions, but his tongue is tied; he has nothing to say; he is in the condition of Doctor Rice's friend who came home drunk and explained it to his wife, and his wife said to him, "John, when you have drunk all the whiskey you want, you ought to ask for sarsaparilla." He said, "Yes, but when I have drunk all the whiskey I want I can't say sarsaparilla." And so I think it is much better to leave a man unmolested until the testimony and pleadings are all in. Otherwise he is dumb—he is at the sarsaparilla stage.

Before I get to the higgledy-piggledy point, as Mr. Howells suggested I do, I want to thank you, gentlemen, for this very high honor you are doing me, and I am quite competent to estimate it at its value. I see around me captains of all the illustrious industries, most distinguished men; there are more than fifty here, and I believe I know thirty-nine of them well. I could probably borrow money from—from the others, anyway. It is a proud thing to me, indeed, to see such a distinguished company gather here on such an occasion as this, when there is no foreign prince to be feted—when you have come here not to do honor to hereditary privilege and ancient lineage, but to do reverence to mere moral excellence and elemental veracity—and, dear me, how old it seems to make me!

I look around me and I see three or four persons I have known so many, many years. I have known Mr. Secretary Hay—John Hay, as the nation and the rest of his friends love to call him—I have known John Hay and Tom Reed and the Reverend Twichell close upon thirty-six years. Close upon thirty-six years I have known those venerable men. I have known Mr. Howells nearly thirty-four years, and I knew Chauncey Depew before he could walk straight, and before he learned to tell the truth. Twenty-seven years ago I heard him make the most noble and eloquent and beautiful speech that has ever fallen from even his capable lips. Tom Reed said that my principal defect was inaccuracy of statement. Well, suppose that that is true. What's the use of telling the truth all the time? I never tell the truth about Tom Reed—but that is his defect, truth; he speaks the truth always. Tom Reed has a good heart, and he has a good intellect, but he hasn't any judgment. Why, when Tom Reed was invited to lecture to the Ladies' Society for the Procreation or Procrastination, or something, of morals, I don't know what it was—advancement, I suppose, of pure morals—he had the immortal indiscretion to begin by saying that some of us can't be optimists, but by judiciously utilizing the opportunities that Providence puts in our way we can all be bigamists. You perceive his limitations. Anything he has in his mind he states, if he thinks it is true. Well, that was true, but that was no place to say it—so they fired him out.

A lot of accounts have been settled here tonight for me; I have held grudges against some of these people, but they have all been wiped out by the very handsome compliments that have been paid me. Even Wayne MacVeagh—I have had a grudge against him many years. The first time I saw Wayne MacVeagh was at a private dinner party at Charles A. Dana's, and when I got there he was clattering along, and I tried to get a word in here and there; but you know what Wayne MacVeagh is when he is started, and I could not get in five words to his one—or one word to his five. I struggled along and struggled along, and—well, I wanted to tell and I was trying to tell a dream I had had the night before, and it was a remarkable dream, a dream worth people's while to listen to, a dream recounting Sam Jones the revivalist's reception in heaven. I was on a train, and was approaching the celestial way-station—I had a through ticket—and I noticed a man sitting alongside of me asleep, and he had his ticket in his hat. He was the remains of the Archbishop of Canterbury; I recognized him by his photograph. I had nothing against him, so I took his ticket and let him have mine. He didn't object—he wasn't in a condition to object—and presently when the train stopped at the heavenly station—well, I got off, and he went on by request—but there they all were, the angels, you know, millions of them, every one with a torch; they had arranged for a torch-light procession; they were expecting the Archbishop, and when I got off they started to raise a shout, but it didn't materialize. I don't know whether they were disappointed. I suppose they had a lot of superstitious ideas about the Archbishop and what he should look like, and I didn't fill the bill, and I was trying to explain to Saint Peter, and was doing it in the German tongue, because I didn't want to be too explicit. Well, I found it was no use, I couldn't get along, for Wayne MacVeagh was occupying the whole place, and I said to Mr. Dana, "What is the matter with that man? Who is that man with the long tongue? What's the trouble with him, that long, lank cadaver, old oil-derrick out of a job—who is that?"

"Well, now," Mr. Dana said, "you don't want to meddle with him; you had better keep quiet; just keep quiet, because that's a bad man. Talk! He was born to talk. Don't let him get out with you; he'll skin you."

I said, "I have been skinned, skinned, and skinned for years, there is nothing left."

He said, "Oh, you'll find there is; that man is the very seed and inspiration of that proverb which says, 'No matter how close you skin an onion, a clever man can always peel it again.'" Well, I reflected and I quieted down. That would never occur to Tom Reed. He's got no discretion. Well, MacVeagh is just the same man; he hasn't changed a bit in all those years; he has been peeling Mr. Mitchell lately. That's the kind of man he is.

Mr. Howells—that poem of his is admirable; that's the way to treat a person. Howells has a peculiar gift for seeing the merits of people, and he has always exhibited them in my favor. Howells has never written anything about me that I couldn't read six or seven times a day; he is always just and always fair; he has written more appreciatively of me than anyone in this world, and published it in the *North American Review*. He did me the justice to say that my intentions—he italicized that—that my intentions were always good, that I wounded people's conventions rather than their convictions. Now, I wouldn't want anything handsomer than that said of me. I would rather wait, with anything harsh I might have to say, till the convictions become conventions.

[John Kendrick] Bangs has traced me all the way down. He can't find that honest man, but I will look for him in the looking-glass when I get home. It was intimated by the Colonel [George Harvey] that it is New England that makes New York and builds up this country and makes it great, overlooking the fact that there's a lot of people here who came from elsewhere, like John Hay from away out West, and Howells from Ohio, and St. Clair McKelway and me from Missouri, and we are doing what we can to build up New York a little—elevate it.

Why, when I was living in that village of Hannibal, Missouri, on the banks of the Mississippi, and Hay up in the town of Warsaw, also on the banks of the Mississippi River—it is an emotional bit of the Mississippi, and when it is low water you have to climb up to it on a ladder, and when it floods you have to hunt for it with a deep-sea lead—but it is a great and beautiful country. In that old time it was a paradise for simplicity—it was a simple, simple life, cheap but comfortable, and full of sweetness, and there was nothing of this rage of modern civilization there at all. It was a delectable land.

I went out there last June, and I met in that town of Hannibal a schoolmate of mine, John Briggs, whom I had not seen for more than fifty years. I tell you, that was a meeting! That pal whom I had known as a little boy long ago, and knew now as a stately man three or four inches over six feet and browned by exposure to many climes, he was back there to see that old place again. We spent a whole afternoon going about here and there and yonder, and hunting up the scenes and talking of the crimes which we had committed so long ago. It was a heartbreaking delight, full of pathos, laughter, and tears, all mixed together; and we called the roll of the boys and girls that we picnicked and sweethearted with so many years ago, and there were hardly half a dozen of them left; the rest were in their graves; and we went up there on the summit of that hill, a treasured place in my memory, the summit of Holiday's Hill, and looked out again over that magnificent panorama of the Mississippi River, sweeping along league after league, a level green paradise on one side, and retreating capes and promontories as far as you could see on the other, fading away in the soft, rich lights of the remote distance. I recognized then that I was seeing now the most enchanting river view the planet could furnish. I never knew it when I was a boy; it took an educated eye that had travelled over the globe to know and appreciate it; and John said, "Can you point out the place where Bear Creek used to be before the railroad came?"

I said, "Yes, it ran along yonder."

"And can you point out the swimming-hole?"

"Yes, out there."

And he said, "Can you point out the place where we stole the skiff?" Well, I didn't know which one he meant. Such a wilderness of events had intervened since that day, more than fifty years ago, it took me more than five minutes to call back that little incident, and then I did call it back; it was a white skiff, and we painted it red to allay suspicion. And the saddest, saddest man came along—a stranger he was—and he looked that red skiff over so pathetically, and he said: "Well, if it weren't for the complexion I'd know whose skiff that was." He said it in that pleading way, you know, that appeals for sympathy and suggestion; we were full of sympathy for him, but we weren't in any condition to offer suggestions. I can see him yet as he turned away with that same sad look on his face and vanished out of history forever. I wonder what became of that man. I know what became of the skiff. Well, it was a beautiful life, a lovely life. There was no crime. Merely little things like pillaging orchards and watermelon-patches and breaking the Sabbath—we didn't break the Sabbath often enough to signify—once a week perhaps. But we were good boys, good Presbyterian boys, all Presbyterian boys, and loyal and all that; anyway, we were good Presbyterian boys when the weather was doubtful; when it was fair, we did wander a little from the fold.

Look at John Hay and me. There we were in obscurity, and look where we are now. Consider the ladder which he has climbed, the illustrious vocations he has served—and vocations is the right word; he has in all those vocations acquitted himself with high credit and honor to his country and to the mother that bore him. Scholar, soldier, diplomat, poet, historian—now, see where we are. He is Secretary of State and I am a gentleman. It could not happen in any other country. Our institutions give men the positions that of right belong to them through merit; all you men have won your places, not by heredities, and not by family influence or extraneous help, but only by the natural gifts God gave you at your birth, made effective by your own energies; this is the country to live in.

Now, there is one invisible guest here. A part of me is present; the larger part, the better part, is yonder at her home; that is my wife, and she has a good many personal friends here, and I think it won't distress any one of them to know that, although she is going to be confined to that bed for many months to come from that nervous prostration, there is not any danger and she is coming along very well—and I think it quite appropriate that I should speak of her. I knew her for the first time just in the same year that I first knew John Hay and Tom Reed and Mr. Twichell—thirty-six years ago—and she has been the best friend I have ever had, and that is saying a good deal; she has reared me, she and Twichell together—and what I am I owe to them.

Twichell—why, it is such a pleasure to look upon Twichell's face! For five-and-twenty years I was under the Rev. Mr. Twichell's tuition, I was in his pastorate, occupying a pew in his church, and held him in due reverence. That man is full of all the graces that go to make a person companionable and beloved; and wherever Twichell goes to start a church the people flock there to buy the land; they find real estate goes up all around the spot, and the envious and the thoughtful always try to get Twichell to move to their neighborhood and start a church; and wherever you see him go you can go and buy land there with confidence, feeling sure that there will be a double price for you before very long. I am not saying this to flatter Mr. Twichell; it is the fact. Many and many a time I have attended the annual sale in his church, and bought up all the pews on a margin—and it would have been better for me spiritually and financially if I had stayed under his wing.

I have tried to do good in this world, and it is marvelous in how many different ways I have done good, and it is comfortable to reflect—now, there's Mr. Rogers—just out of the affection I bear that man many a time I have given him points in finance that he had never thought of—and if he could lay aside envy, prejudice, and superstition, and utilize those ideas in his business, it would make a difference in his bank account.

Well, I like the poetry. I like all the speeches and the poetry, too. I liked Doctor Van Dyke's poem. I wish I could return thanks in proper measure to you, gentlemen, who have spoken and violated your feelings to pay me compliments; some were merited and some you overlooked, it is true; and Colonel Harvey did slander every one of you, and put things into my mouth that I never said, never thought of at all.

And now, my wife and I, out of our single heart, return you our deepest and most grateful thanks, and—yesterday was her birthday.

SEVENTIETH BIRTHDAY

New York City, December 5, 1905

Twain's birthday was November 30, which was greeted with an outpouring of good wishes from his friends and admirers. Colonel George Harvey gave the dinner at Delmonico's Restaurant. William Dean Howells introduced his friend: "Now, ladies and gentlemen, and Colonel Harvey, I will try not to be greedy on your behalf in wishing the health of our honored and, in view of his great age, our revered guest. I will not say, 'Oh King, live forever!' but 'Oh King, live as long as you like!'"

Well, if I made that joke, it is the best one I ever made, and it is in the prettiest language, too. I never can get quite to that height. But I appreciate that joke, and I shall remember it—and I shall use it when occasion requires.

I have had a great many birthdays in my time. I remember the first one very well, and I always think of it with indignation; everything was so crude, unaesthetic, primeval. Nothing like this at all. No proper appreciative preparation made; nothing really ready. Now, for a person born with high and delicate instincts—why, even the cradle wasn't whitewashed—nothing ready at all. I hadn't any hair, I hadn't any teeth, I hadn't any clothes, I had to go to my first banquet just like that. Well, everybody came swarming in. It was the merest little bit of a village—hardly that, just a little hamlet, in the backwoods of Missouri, where nothing ever happened, and the people were all interested, and they all came; they looked me over to see if there was anything fresh in my line. Why, nothing ever happened in that village—I—why, I was the only thing that had really happened there for months and months and months; and although I say it myself that shouldn't, I came the nearest to being a real event that had happened in that village in more than two years. Well, those people came, they came with that curiosity which is so provincial, with that frankness which also is so provincial, and they examined me all around and gave their opinion. Nobody asked them, and I shouldn't have minded if anybody had paid me a compliment, but nobody did. Their opinions were all just green with prejudice, and I feel those opinions to this day. Well, I stood that as long as—well, you know I was born courteous and I stood it to the limit. I stood it an hour, and then the worm turned. I was the worm; it was my turn to turn, and I turned. I knew very well the strength of my position; I knew that I was the only spotlessly pure and innocent person in that whole town, and I came out and said so. And they could not say a word. It was so true, they blushed; they were embarrassed. Well, that was the first after-dinner speech I ever made. I think it was after dinner.

It's a long stretch between that first birthday speech and this one. That was my cradle-song, and this is my swan-song, I suppose. I am used to swan-songs; I have sung them several times.

This is my seventieth birthday, and I wonder if you all rise to the size of that proposition, realizing all the significance of that phrase, seventieth birthday.

The seventieth birthday! It is the time of life when you arrive at a new and awful dignity; when you may throw aside the decent reserves which have oppressed you for a generation and stand unafraid and unabashed upon your seven-terraced summit and look down and teach—unrebuked. You can tell the world how you got there. It is what they all do. You shall never get tired of telling by what delicate arts and deep moralities you climbed up to that great place. You will explain the process and dwell on the particulars with senile rapture. I have been anxious to explain my own system this long time, and now at last I have the right.

I have achieved my seventy years in the usual way: by sticking strictly to a scheme of life which would kill anybody else. It sounds like an exaggeration, but that is really the common rule for attaining to old age. When we examine the program of any of these garrulous old people we always find that the habits which have preserved them would have decayed us; that the way of life which enabled them to live upon the property of their heirs so long, as Mr. Choate says, would have put us out of commission ahead of time. I will offer here, as a sound maxim, this: That we can't reach old age by another man's road.

I will now teach, offering my way of life to whomsoever desires to commit suicide by the scheme which has enabled me to beat the doctor and the hangman for seventy years. Some of the details may sound untrue, but they are not. I am not here to deceive; I am here to teach.

We have no permanent habits until we are forty. Then they begin to harden, presently they petrify, then business begins. Since forty I have been regular about going to bed and getting up-and that is one of the main things. I have made it a rule to go to bed when there wasn't anybody left to sit up with; and I have made it a rule to get up when I had to. This has resulted in an unswerving regularity of irregularity. It has saved me sound, but it would injure another person.

In the matter of diet—which is another main thing—I have been persistently strict in sticking to the things which didn't agree with me until one or the other of us got the best of it. Until lately I got the best of it myself. But last spring I stopped frolicking with mince-pie after midnight; up to then I had always believed it wasn't loaded. For thirty years I have taken coffee and bread at eight in the morning, and no bite nor sup until seven-thirty in the evening. Eleven hours. That is all right for me, and is wholesome, because I have never had a headache in my life, but headachy people would not reach seventy comfortably by that road, and they would be foolish to try it. And I wish to urge upon you this—which I think is wisdom—that if you find you can't make seventy by any but an uncomfortable road, don't you go. When they take off the Pullman and retire you to the rancid smoker, put on your things, count your checks, and get out at the first way station where there's a cemetery.

I have made it a rule never to smoke more than one cigar at a time. I have no other restriction as regards smoking. I do not know just when I began to smoke, I only know that it was in my father's lifetime, and that I was discreet. He passed from this life early in 1847, when I was a shade past eleven; ever since then I have smoked publicly. As an example to others, and not that I care for moderation myself, it has always been my rule never to smoke when asleep, and never to refrain when awake. It is a good rule. I mean, for me; but some of you know quite well that it wouldn't answer for everybody that's trying to get to be seventy.

I smoke in bed until I have to go to sleep; I wake up in the night, sometimes once, sometimes twice, sometimes three times, and I never waste any of these opportunities to smoke. This habit is so old and dear and precious to me that I would feel as you, sir, would feel if you should lose the only moral you've got—meaning the chairman—if you've got one: I am making no charges. I will grant, here, that I have stopped smoking now and then, for a few months at a time, but it was not on principle, it was only to show off; it was to pulverize those critics who said I was a slave to my habits and couldn't break my bonds.

Today it is all of sixty years since I began to smoke the limit. I have never bought cigars with life-belts around them. I early found that those were too expensive for me. I have always bought cheap cigars—reasonably cheap, at any rate. Sixty years ago they cost me four dollars a barrel, but my taste has improved, latterly, and I pay seven now. Six or seven. Seven, I think. Yes, it's seven. But that includes the barrel. I often have smoking parties at my house; but the people that come have always just taken the pledge. I wonder why that is?

As for drinking, I have no rule about that. When the others drink I like to help; otherwise I remain dry, by habit and preference. This dryness does not hurt me, but it could easily hurt you, because you are different. You let it alone.

Since I was seven years old I have seldom taken a dose of medicine, and have still seldomer needed one. But up to seven I lived exclusively on allopathic medicines. Not that I needed them, for I don't think I did; it was for economy; my father took a drugstore for a debt, and it made cod-liver oil cheaper than the other breakfast foods. We had nine barrels of it, and it lasted me seven years. Then I was weaned. The rest of the family had to get along with rhubarb and ipecac and such things, because I was the pet. I was the first Standard Oil Trust. I had it all. By the time the drug store was exhausted my health was established, and there has never been much the matter with, me since. But you know very well it would be foolish for the average child to start for seventy on that basis. It happened to be just the thing for me, but that was merely an accident; it couldn't happen again in a century.

I have never taken any exercise, except sleeping and resting, and I never intend to take any. Exercise is loathsome. And it cannot be any benefit when you are tired; and I was always tired. But let another person try my way, and see where he will come out.

I desire now to repeat and emphasize that maxim: We can't reach old age by another man's road. My habits protect my life, but they would assassinate you.

I have lived a severely moral life. But it would be a mistake for other people to try that, or for me to recommend it. Very few would succeed: you have to have a perfectly colossal stock of morals; and you can't get them on a margin; you have to have the whole thing, and put them in your box. Morals are an acquirement—like music, like a foreign language, like piety, poker, paralysis—no man is born with them. I wasn't myself, I started poor. I hadn't a single moral. There is hardly a man in this house that is poorer than I was then. Yes, I started like that—the world before me, not a moral in the slot. Not even an insurance moral. I can remember the first one I ever got. I can remember the landscape, the weather, the—I can remember how everything looked. It was an old moral, an old second-hand moral, all out of repair, and didn't fit, anyway. But if you are careful with a thing like that, and keep it in a dry place, and save it for processions, and Chautauquas, and World's Fairs, and so on, and disinfect it now and then, and give it a fresh coat of whitewash once in a while, you will be surprised to see how well she will last and how long she will keep sweet, or at least inoffensive.

When I got that moldy old moral, she had stopped growing, because she hadn't any exercise; but I worked her hard, I worked her Sundays and all. Under this cultivation she waxed in might and stature beyond belief, and served me well and was my pride and joy for sixty-three years; then she got to associating with insurance presidents, and lost flesh and character, and was a sorrow to look at and no longer competent for business. She was a great loss to me. Yet not all loss. I sold her—ah, pathetic skeleton, as she was—I sold her to Leopold, the pirate King of Belgium; he sold her to our Metropolitan Museum, and it was very glad to get her, for without a rag on, she stands 57 feet long and 16 feet high, and they think she's a brontosaur. Well, she looks it. They believe it will take nineteen geological periods to breed her match.

Morals are of inestimable value, for every man is born crammed with sin microbes, and the only thing that can extirpate these sin microbes is morals. Now you take a sterilized Christian—I mean, you take *the* sterilized Christian, for there's only one. Dear sir, I wish you wouldn't look at me like that.

Threescore years and ten!

It is the Scriptural statute of limitations. After that, you owe no active duties; for you the strenuous life is over. You are a time-expired man, to use Kipling's military phrase: You have served your term, well or less well, and you are mustered out. You are become an honorary member of the republic, you are emancipated, compulsions are not for you, not any bugle-call but "lights out." You pay the time-worn duty bills if you choose, or decline if you prefer—and without prejudice— for they are not legally collectable.

The previous-engagement plea, which in forty years has cost you so many twinges, you can lay aside forever; on this side of the grave you will never need it again. If you shrink at the thought of night and winter, and the late home-coming from the banquet and the lights and the laughter through the deserted streets—a desolation which would not remind you now, as for a generation it did, that your friends are sleeping, and you must creep in a-tiptoe and not disturb them, but would only remind you that you need not tiptoe, you can never disturb them more—if you shrink at thought of these things, you need only reply, "Your invitation honors me, and pleases me because you still keep me in your remembrance, but I am seventy; seventy, and would nestle in the chimney-corner, and smoke my pipe, and read my book, and take my rest, wishing you well in all affection, and that when you in your return shall arrive at pier No. 70 you may step aboard your waiting ship with a reconciled spirit, and lay your course toward the sinking sun with a contented heart."

RUSSIAN JEWISH SUFFERERS

New York City, December 18, 1905

After the failed Russian Revolution of 1905, the Russian government stepped up its violent repression of Jews in St. Petersburg and Moscow. Twain appeared at a benefit with Broadway stars and famous French actress Sarah Bernhardt.

Ladies and Gentlemen,

It seems a sort of cruelty to inflict upon an audience like this our rude English tongue, after we have heard that divine speech flowing in that lucid Gallic tongue.

It has always been a marvel to me—that French language; it has always been a puzzle to me. How beautiful that language is. How expressive it seems to be. How full of grace it is.

And when it comes from lips like those, how eloquent and how liquid it is. And, oh, I am always deceived—I always think I am going to understand it.

Oh, it is such a delight to me, such a delight to me, to meet Madame Bernhardt, and laugh hand to hand and heart to heart with her.

I have seen her play, as we all have, and oh, that is divine; but I have always wanted to know Madame Bernhardt herself—her fiery self. I have wanted to know that beautiful character.

Why, she is the youngest person I ever saw, except myself—for I always feel young when I come in the presence of young people.

I have a pleasant recollection of an incident so many years ago— when Madame Bernhardt came to Hartford, where I lived, and she was going to play and the tickets were three dollars, and there were two lovely women—a widow and her daughter—neighbors of ours, highly cultivated ladies they were; their tastes were fine and elevated, but they were very poor, and they said: "Well, we must not spend six dollars on a pleasure of the mind, a pleasure of the intellect; we must spend it, if it must go at all, to furnish to somebody bread to eat."

And so they sorrowed over the fact that they had to give up that great pleasure of seeing Madame Bernhardt, but there were two neighbors equally highly cultivated and who could not afford bread, and those good-hearted Joneses sent that six dollars—deprived themselves of it—and sent it to those poor Smiths to buy bread with. And those Smiths took it and bought tickets with it to see Madame Bernhardt.

Oh yes, some people have tastes and intelligence also.

Now, I was going to make a speech—I supposed I was, but I am not. It is late, late; and so I am going to tell a story; and there is this advantage about a story, anyway, that whatever moral or valuable thing you put into a speech, why, it gets diffused among those involuted sentences and possibly your audience goes away without finding out what that valuable thing was that you were trying to confer upon it; but, dear me, you put the same jewel into a story and it becomes the keystone of that story, and you are bound to get it—it flashes, it flames, it is the jewel in the toad's head-you don't overlook that.

Now, if I am going to talk on such a subject as, for instance, the lost opportunity—oh, the lost opportunity. Anybody in this house who has reached the turn of life—sixty or seventy, or even fifty, or along there—when he goes back along his history, there he finds it mile-stoned all the way with the lost opportunity, and you know how pathetic that is.

You younger ones cannot know the full pathos that lies in those words—the lost opportunity; but anybody who is old, who has really lived and felt this life, he knows the pathos of the lost opportunity.

Now, I will tell you a story whose moral is that, whose lesson is that, whose lament is that.

I was in a village which is a suburb of New Bedford several years ago—well, New Bedford is a suburb of Fair Haven, or perhaps it is the other way; in any case, it took both of those towns to make a great center of the great whaling industry of the first half of the nineteenth century, and I was up there at Fair Haven some years ago with a friend of mine.

There was a dedication of a great town-hall, a public building, and we were there in the afternoon. This great building was filled, like this great theater, with rejoicing villagers, and my friend and I started down the centre aisle. He saw a man standing in that aisle, and he said:

"Now, look at that bronzed veteran—at that mahogany-faced man. Now, tell me, do you see anything about that man's face that is emotional? Do you see anything about it that suggests that inside that man anywhere there are fires that can be started? Would you ever imagine that that is a human volcano?"

"Why, no," I said, "I would not. He looks like a wooden Indian in front of a cigar store."

"Very well," said my friend, "I will show you that there is emotion even in that unpromising place. I will just go to that man and I will just mention in the most casual way an incident in his life. That man is getting along toward ninety years old. He is past eighty. I will mention an incident of fifty or sixty years ago. Now, just watch the effect, and it will be so casual that if you don't watch you won't know when I do say that thing—but you just watch the effect."

He went on down there and accosted this antiquity, and made a remark or two. I could not catch up. They were so casual I could not recognize which one it was that touched that bottom, for in an instant that old man was literally in eruption and was filling the whole place with profanity of the most exquisite kind. You never heard such accomplished profanity. I never heard it also delivered with such eloquence.

I never enjoyed profanity as I enjoyed it then—more than if I had been uttering it myself. There is nothing like listening to an artist—all his passions passing away in lava, smoke, thunder, lightning, and earthquake.

Then this friend said to me: "Now, I will tell you about that. About sixty years ago that man was a young fellow of twenty-three, and had just come home from a three years' whaling voyage. He came into that village of his, happy and proud because now, instead of being chief mate, he was going to be master of a whaleship, and he was proud and happy about it.

"Then he found that there had been a kind of a cold frost come upon that town and the whole region roundabout; for while he had been away the Father Mathew temperance excitement had come upon the whole region. Therefore, everybody had taken the pledge; there wasn't anybody for miles and miles around that had not taken the pledge.

"So you can see what a solitude it was to this young man, who was fond of his grog. And he was just an outcast, because when they found he would not join Father Mathew's Society they ostracized him, and he went about that town three weeks, day and night, in utter loneliness—the only human being in the whole place who ever took grog, and he had to take it privately.

"If you don't know what it is to be ostracized, to be shunned by your fellow-man, may you never know it. Then he recognized that there was something more valuable in this life than grog, and that is the fellowship of your fellow-man. And at last he gave it up, and at nine o'clock one night he went down to the Father Mathew Temperance Society, and with a broken heart he said: 'Put my name down for membership in this society.'

"And then he went away crying, and at earliest dawn the next morning they came for him and routed him out, and they said that new ship of his was ready to sail on a three years' voyage. In a minute he was on board that ship and gone.

"And he said—well, he was not out of sight of that town till he began to repent, but he had made up his mind that he would not take a drink, and so that whole voyage of three years was a three years' agony to that man because he saw all the time the mistake he had made.

"He felt it all through; he had constant reminders of it, because the crew would pass him with their grog, come out on the deck and take it, and there was the torturous smell of it.

"He went through the whole three years of suffering, and at last coming into port it was snowy, it was cold, he was stamping through the snow two feet deep on the deck and longing to get home, and there was his crew torturing him to the last minute with hot grog, but at last he had his reward. He really did get to shore at last, and jumped and ran and bought a jug and rushed to the society's office, and said to the secretary:

"'Take my name off your membership books, and do it right away! I have got a three years' thirst on.'

"And the secretary said: 'It is not necessary. You were blackballed!'"

JOAN OF ARC

New York City, December 21, 1905

Twain spoke at a dinner of the Society of Illustrators. Howells writes: "Just before Mr. Clemens made his speech, a young woman attired as Joan of Arc, with a page bearing her flag of battle, courtsied reverently and tendered Mr. Clemens a laurel wreath on a satin pillow. He tried to speak, but his voice failed from excess of emotion. 'I thank you!' he finally exclaimed, and, pulling himself together, he began his speech." Of all the women in history, Twain most revered Joan of Arc and Helen Keller. He often said his own favorite book was his biography of Joan of Arc. (Few readers have ever shared that assessment.)

Now there is an illustration *[pointing to the retreating Joan of Arc]*. That is exactly what I wanted—precisely what I wanted—when I was describing to myself Joan of Arc, after studying her history and her character for twelve years diligently.

That was the product—not the conventional Joan of Arc. Wherever you find the conventional Joan of Arc in history she is an offence to anybody who knows the story of that wonderful girl.

Why, she was—she was almost supreme in several details. She had a marvelous intellect; she had a great heart, had a noble spirit, was absolutely pure in her character, her feeling, her language, her words, her everything—she was only eighteen years old.

Now put that heart into such a breast—eighteen years old—and give it that masterly intellect which showed in the fate, and furnish it with that almost god-like spirit, and what are you going to have? The conventional Joan of Arc? Not by any means. That is impossible. I cannot comprehend any such thing as that.

You must have a creature like that young and fair and beautiful girl we just saw. And her spirit must look out of the eyes. The figure should be—the figure should be in harmony with all that, but, oh, what we get in the conventional picture, and it is always the conventional picture!

I hope you will allow me to say that your guild, when you take the conventional, you have got it at second-hand. Certainly, if you had studied and studied, then you might have something else as a result, but when you have the common convention you stick to that.

You cannot prevail upon the artist to do it; he always gives you a Joan of Arc—that lovely creature that started a great career at thirteen, but whose greatness arrived when she was eighteen; and merely because she was a girl he cannot see the divinity in her, and so he paints a peasant, a coarse and lubberly figure—the figure of a cotton-bale, and he clothes that in the coarsest raiment of the peasant region—just like a fish-woman, her hair cropped short like a Russian peasant, and that face of hers, which should be beautiful and which should radiate all the glories which are in the spirit and in her heart—that expression in that face is always just the fixed expression of a ham.

But now Mr. Beard has intimated a moment ago, and so has Sir Purdon-Clarke also, that the artist, the illustrator, does not often get the idea of the man whose book he is illustrating. Here is a very remarkable instance of the other thing in Mr. Beard, who illustrated a book of mine. You may never have heard of it. I will tell you about it now— *A Yankee in King Arthur's Court.*

Now, Beard got everything that I put into that book and a little more besides. Those pictures of Beard's in that book—oh, from the first page to the last is one vast sardonic laugh at the trivialities, the servilities of our poor human race, and also at the professions and the insolence of priest-craft and king-craft—those creatures that make slaves of themselves and have not the manliness to shake it off. Beard put it all in that book. I meant it to be there. I put a lot of it there and Beard put the rest.

That publisher of mine in Hartford had an eye for the pennies, and he saved them. He did not waste any on the illustrations. He had a very good artist—Williams—who had never taken a lesson in drawing. Everything he did was original. The publisher hired the cheapest wood-engraver he could find, and in my early books you can see a trace of that. You can see that if Williams had had a chance he would have made some very good pictures. He had a good heart and good intentions.

I had a character in the first book he illustrated—*The Innocents Abroad.* That was a boy seventeen or eighteen years old—Jack Van Nostrand—a New York boy, who, to my mind, was a very remarkable creature. He and I tried to get Williams to understand that boy, and make a picture of Jack that would be worthy of Jack.

Jack was a most singular combination. He was born and reared in New York here. He was as delicate in his feelings, as clean and pure and refined in his feelings as any lovely girl that ever was, but whenever he expressed a feeling he did it in Bowery slang, and it was a most curious combination—that delicacy of his and that apparent coarseness. There was no coarseness inside of Jack at all, and Jack, in the course of seventeen or eighteen years, had acquired a capital of ignorance that was marvelous—ignorance of various things, not of all things. For instance, he did not know anything about the Bible. He had never been in Sunday-school. Jack got more out of the Holy Land than anybody else, because the others knew what they were expecting, but it was a land of surprises to him.

I said in the book that we found him watching a turtle on a log, stoning that turtle, and he was stoning that turtle because he had read that "The song of the turtle was heard in the land," and this turtle wouldn't sing. It sounded absurd, but it was charged on Jack as a fact, and as he went along through that country he had a proper foil in an old rebel colonel, who was superintendent and head engineer in a large Sunday-school in Wheeling, West Virginia. That man was full of enthusiasm wherever he went, and would stand and deliver himself of speeches, and Jack would listen to those speeches of the colonel and wonder.

Jack had made a trip as a child almost across this continent in the first overland stagecoach. That man's name who ran that line of stages— well, I declare that name is gone. Well, names will go.

Halliday—ah, that's the name—Ben Halliday, your uncle *[turning to Mr. Andrew Carnegie]*. That was the fellow—Ben Halliday—and Jack was full of admiration at the prodigious speed that that line of stages made—and it was good speed—one hundred and twenty-five miles a day, going day and night, and it was the event of Jack's life, and there at the Fords of the Jordan the colonel was inspired to a speech (he was always making a speech), so he called us up to him. He called up five sinners and three saints. It has been only lately that Mr. Carnegie beatified me. And he said: "Here are the Fords of the Jordan—a monumental place. At this very point, when Moses brought the children of Israel through—he brought the children of Israel from Egypt through the desert you see there—he guarded them through that desert patiently, patiently during forty years, and brought them to this spot safe and sound. There you see—there is the scene of what Moses did."

And Jack said: "Moses who?"

"Oh," he says, "Jack, you ought not to ask that! Moses, the great law-giver! Moses, the great patriot! Moses, the great warrior! Moses, the great guide, who, as I tell you, brought these people through these three hundred miles of sand in forty years, and landed them safe and sound."

Jack said: "There's nothin' in that three hundred miles in forty years. Ben Halliday would have snaked 'em through in thirty-six hours."

Well, I was speaking of Jack's innocence, and it was beautiful. Jack was not ignorant on all subjects. That boy was a deep student in the history of Anglo-Saxon liberty, and he was a patriot all the way through to the marrow. There was a subject that interested him all the time. Other subjects were of no concern to Jack, but that quaint, inscrutable innocence of his I could not get Williams to put into the picture.

Yes, Williams wanted to do it. He said: "I will make him as innocent as a virgin." He thought a moment, and then said, "I will make him as innocent as an unborn virgin," which covered the ground.

I was reminded of Jack because I came across a letter today which is over thirty years old that Jack wrote. Jack was doomed to consumption. He was very long and slim, poor creature, and in a year or two after he got back from that excursion to the Holy Land he went on a ride on horseback through Colorado, and he did not last but a year or two.

He wrote this letter, not to me, but to a friend of mine, and he said: "I have ridden horseback"—this was three years after—"I have ridden horseback four hundred miles through a desert country where you never see anything but cattle now and then, and now and then a cattle station—ten miles apart, twenty miles apart. Now you tell Clemens that in all that stretch of four hundred miles I have seen only two books—the Bible and *Innocents Abroad*. Tell Clemens the Bible was in a very good condition."

I say that he had studied, and he had, the real Saxon liberty, the acquirement of our liberty, and Jack used to repeat some verses—I don't know where they came from, but I thought of them today when I saw that letter—that that boy could have been talking of himself in those quoted lines from that unknown poet:

> For he had sat at Sidney's feet
> And walked with him in plain apart,
> And through the centuries heard the beat
> Of Freedom's march through Cromwell's heart.

And he was that kind of a boy. He should have lived, and yet he should not have lived, because he died at that early age—he couldn't have been more than twenty—he had seen all there was to see in the world that was worth the trouble of living in it; he had seen all of this world that is valuable; he had seen all of this world that was illusion, and illusion is the only valuable thing in it. He had arrived at that point where presently the illusions would cease and he would have entered upon the realities of life, and God help the man that has arrived at that point.

TAXES AND MORALS

New York City, January 22, 1906

At a fundraiser and meeting at Carnegie Hall commemorating the twenty-fifth anniversary of the founding of Tuskeegee Institute by Booker T. Washington, the lawyer and former ambassador Joseph H. Choate presided. William Dean Howells writes: "In introducing" Twain, Choate "made fun of him because he made play his work, and that when he worked hardest he did so lying in bed."

I came here in the responsible capacity of policeman to watch Mr. Choate. This is an occasion of grave and serious importance, and it seems necessary for me to be present, so that if he tried to work off any statement that required correction, reduction, refutation, or exposure, there would be a tried friend of the public to protect the house. He has not made one statement whose veracity fails to tally exactly with my own standard. I have never seen a person improve so. This makes me thankful and proud of a country that can produce such men—two such men. And all in the same country. We can't be with you always; we are passing away, and then—well, everything will have to stop, I reckon. It is a sad thought. But in spirit I shall still be with you. Choate, too—if he can.

Every born American among the eighty millions, let his creed or destitution of creed be what it may, is indisputably a Christian to this degree—that his moral constitution is Christian.

There are two kinds of Christian morals, one private and the other public. These two are so distinct, so unrelated, that they are no more akin to each other than are archangels and politicians. During three hundred and sixty-three days in the year the American citizen is true to his Christian private morals, and keeps undefiled the nation's character at its best and highest; then in the other two days of the year he leaves his Christian private morals at home and carries his Christian public morals to the tax office and the polls, and does the best he can to damage and undo his whole year's faithful and righteous work. Without a blush he will vote for an unclean boss if that boss is his party's Moses, without compunction he will vote against the best man in the whole land if he is on the other ticket. Every year in a number of cities and States he helps put corrupt men in office, whereas if he would but throw away his Christian public morals, and carry his Christian private morals to the polls, he could promptly purify the public service and make the possession of office a high and honorable distinction.

Once a year he lays aside his Christian private morals and hires a ferry-boat and piles up his bonds in a warehouse in New Jersey for three days, and gets out his Christian public morals and goes to the tax office and holds up his hands and swears he wishes he may never never if he's got a cent in the world, so help him. The next day the list appears in the papers—a column and a quarter of names, in fine print, and every man in the list a billionaire and member of a couple of churches. I know all those people. I have friendly, social, and criminal relations with the whole lot of them. They never miss a sermon when they are so's to be around, and they never miss swearing-off day, whether they are so's to be around or not.

I used to be an honest man. I am crumbling. No—I have crumbled. When they assessed me at $75,000 a fortnight ago I went out and tried to borrow the money, and couldn't; then when I found they were letting a whole crop of millionaires live in New York at a third of the price they were charging me. I was hurt, I was indignant, and said: "This is the last feather. I am not going to run this town all by myself." In that moment—in that memorable moment—I began to crumble. In fifteen minutes the disintegration was complete. In fifteen minutes I had become just a mere moral sand-pile; and I lifted up my hand along with those seasoned and experienced deacons and swore off every rag of personal property I've got in the world, clear down to cork leg, glass eye, and what is left of my wig.

Those tax officers were moved; they were profoundly moved. They had long been accustomed to seeing hardened old grafters act like that, and they could endure the spectacle; but they were expecting better things of me, a chartered, professional moralist, and they were saddened. I fell visibly in their respect and esteem, and I should have fallen in my own, except that I had already struck bottom, and there wasn't any place to fall to.

At Tuskeegee they will jump to misleading conclusions from insufficient evidence, along with Doctor Parkhurst, and they will deceive the student with the superstition that no gentleman ever swears.

Look at those good millionaires; aren't they gentlemen? Well, they swear. Only once in a year, maybe, but there's enough bulk to it to make up for the lost time. And do they lose anything by it? No, they don't; they save enough in three minutes to support the family seven years. When they swear, do we shudder? No—unless they say "damn!" Then we do. It shrivels us all up. Yet we ought not to feel so about it, because we all swear—everybody. Including the ladies. Including Doctor Parkhurst, that strong and brave and excellent citizen, but superficially educated.

For it is not the word that is the sin, it is the spirit back of the word. When an irritated lady says "oh!" the spirit back of it is "damn!" and that is the way it is going to be recorded against her. It always makes me so sorry when I hear a lady swear like that. But if she says "damn," and says it in an amiable, nice way, it isn't going to be recorded at all.

The idea that no gentleman ever swears is all wrong; he can swear and still be a gentleman if he does it in a nice and benevolent and affectionate way. The historian, John Fiske, whom I knew well and loved, was a spotless and most noble and upright Christian gentleman, and yet he swore once. Not exactly that, maybe; still, he—but I will tell you about it.

One day, when he was deeply immersed in his work, his wife came in, much moved and profoundly distressed, and said: "I am sorry to disturb you, John, but I must, for this is a serious matter, and needs to be attended to at once." Then, lamenting, she brought a grave accusation against their little son. She said: "He has been saying his Aunt Mary is a fool and his Aunt Martha is a damned fool." Mr. Fiske reflected upon the matter a minute, then said: "Oh, well, it's about the distinction I should make between them myself."

Mr. Washington, I beg you to convey these teachings to your great and prosperous and most beneficent educational institution, and add them to the prodigal mental and moral riches wherewith you equip your fortunate proteges for the struggle of life.

LAYMAN'S SERMON

New York City, March 4, 1906

Twain delivered a "lay sermon" to the West Side Young Men's Christian Association at the Majestic Theatre. So many people tried to get in and snarled traffic that the police saw fit to clear the crowd. Doctor Charles P. Fagnani, introducing Twain, mentioned the overzealousness of the police intervention.

I have been listening to what was said here, and there is in it a lesson of citizenship. You created the police, and you are responsible for them. One must pause, therefore, before criticizing them too harshly. They are citizens, just as we are. A little of citizenship ought to be taught at the mother's knee and in the nursery. Citizenship is what makes a republic; monarchies can get along without it. What keeps a republic on its legs is good citizenship.

Organization is necessary in all things. It is even necessary in reform. I was an organization myself once—for twelve hours. I was in Chicago a few years ago about to depart for New York. There were with me Mr. Osgood, a publisher, and a stenographer. I picked out a state-room on a train, the principal feature of which was that it contained the privilege of smoking. The train had started but a short time when the conductor came in and said that there had been a mistake made, and asked that we vacate the apartment. I refused, but when I went out on the platform Osgood and the stenographer agreed to accept a section. They were too modest.

Now, I am not modest. I was born modest, but it didn't last. I asserted myself, insisted upon my rights, and finally the Pullman conductor and the train conductor capitulated, and I was left in possession.

I went into the dining-car the next morning for breakfast. Ordinarily I only care for coffee and rolls, but this particular morning I espied an important-looking man on the other side of the car eating broiled chicken. I asked for broiled chicken, and I was told by the waiter and later by the dining-car conductor that there was no broiled chicken. There must have been an argument, for the Pullman conductor came in and remarked: "If he wants broiled chicken, give it to him. If you haven't got it on the train, stop somewhere. It will be better for all concerned!" I got the chicken.

It is from experiences such as these that you get your education of life, and you string them into jewels or into tin-ware, as you may choose. I have received recently several letters asking my counsel or advice. The principal request is for some incident that may prove helpful to the young. There were a lot of incidents in my career to help me along—sometimes they helped me along faster than I wanted to go.

Here is such a request. It is a telegram from Joplin, Missouri, and it reads: "In what one of your works can we find the definition of a gentleman?"

I have not answered that telegram, either; I couldn't. It seems to me that if any man has just merciful and kindly instincts he would be a gentleman, for he would need nothing else in the world.

I received the other day a letter from my old friend, William Dean Howells—Howells, the head of American literature. No one is able to stand with him. He is an old, old friend of mine, and he writes me, "Tomorrow I shall be sixty-nine years old." Why, I am surprised at Howells writing that! I have known him longer than that. I'm sorry to see a man trying to appear so young. Let's see. Howells says now, "I see you have been burying Patrick. I suppose he was old, too."

No, he was never old—Patrick. He came to us thirty-six years ago. He was my coachman on the morning that I drove my young bride to our new home. He was a young Irishman, slender, tall, lithe, honest, truthful, and he never changed in all his life. He really was with us but twenty-five years, for he did not go with us to Europe, but he never regarded that as separation. As the children grew up he was their guide. He was all honor, honesty, and affection. He was with us in New Hampshire, with us last summer, and his hair was just as black, his eyes were just as blue, his form just as straight, and his heart just as good as on the day we first met. In all the long years Patrick never made a mistake. He never needed an order, he never received a command. He knew. I have been asked for my idea of an ideal gentleman, and I give it to you—Patrick McAleer.

MORALS AND MEMORY

New York City, March 7, 1906

Barnard College made Twain its guest of honor at a reception by the Barnard Union. Howells (or F. A. Nast) writes: "One of the young ladies presented Mr. Clemens, and thanked him for his amiability in coming to make them an address. She closed with the expression of the great joy it gave her fellow-collegians, 'because we all love you.'"

If anyone here loves me, she has my sincere thanks. Nay, if anyone here is so good as to love me—why, I'll be a brother to her. She shall have my sincere, warm, unsullied affection. When I was coming up in the car with the very kind young lady who was delegated to show me the way, she asked me what I was going to talk about. And I said I wasn't sure. I said I had some illustrations, and I was going to bring them in. I said I was certain to give those illustrations, but that I hadn't the faintest notion what they were going to illustrate.

Now, I've been thinking it over in this forest glade *[indicating the woods of Arcady on the scene setting],* and I've decided to work them in with something about morals and the caprices of memory. That seems to me to be a pretty good subject. You see, everybody has a memory and it's pretty sure to have caprices. And, of course, everybody has morals.

It's my opinion that everyone I know has morals, though I wouldn't like to ask. I know I have. But I'd rather teach them than practice them any day. "Give them to others"—that's my motto. Then you never have any use for them when you're left without. Now, speaking of the caprices of memory in general, and of mine in particular, it's strange to think of all the tricks this little mental process plays on us. Here we're endowed with a faculty of mind that ought to be more supremely serviceable to us than them all. And what happens? This memory of ours stores up a perfect record of the most useless facts and anecdotes and experiences. And all the things that we ought to know—that we

111

need to know—that we'd profit by knowing—it casts aside with the careless indifference of a girl refusing her true lover. It's terrible to think of this phenomenon. I tremble in all my members when I consider all the really valuable things that I've forgotten in seventy years—when I meditate upon the caprices of my memory.

There's a bird out in California that is one perfect symbol of the human memory. I've forgotten the bird's name (just because it would be valuable for me to know it—to recall it to your own minds, perhaps).

But this fool of a creature goes around collecting the most ridiculous things you can imagine and storing them up. He never selects a thing that could ever prove of the slightest help to him; but he goes about gathering iron forks, and spoons, and tin cans, and broken mouse-traps—all sorts of rubbish that is difficult for him to carry and yet be any use when he gets it. Why, that bird will go by a gold watch to bring back one of those patent cake-pans.

Now, my mind is just like that, and my mind isn't very different from yours—and so our minds are just like that bird. We pass by what would be of inestimable value to us, and pack our memories with the most trivial odds and ends that never by any chance, under any circumstances whatsoever, could be of the slightest use to anyone.

Now, things that I have remembered are constantly popping into my head. And I am repeatedly startled by the vividness with which they recur to me after the lapse of years and their utter uselessness in being remembered at all.

I was thinking over some on my way up here. They were the illustrations I spoke about to the young lady on the way up. And I've come to the conclusion, curious though it is, that I can use every one of these freaks of memory to teach you all a lesson. I'm convinced that each one has its moral. And I think it's my duty to hand the moral on to you.

Now, I recall that when I was a boy I was a good boy—I was a very good boy. Why, I was the best boy in my school. I was the best boy in that little Mississippi town where I lived. The population was only about twenty million. You may not believe it, but I was the best boy in that State—and in the United States, for that matter.

But I don't know why I never heard any one say that but myself. I always recognized it. But even those nearest and dearest to me couldn't seem to see it. My mother, especially, seemed to think there was something wrong with that estimate. And she never got over that prejudice.

Now, when my mother got to be eighty-five years old her memory failed her. She forgot little threads that hold life's patches of meaning together. She was living out West then, and I went on to visit her.

I hadn't seen my mother in a year or so. And when I got there she knew my face; knew I was married; knew I had a family, and that I was living, with them. But she couldn't, for the life of her, tell my name or who I was. So I told her I was her boy.

"But you don't live with me," she said.

"No," said I, "I'm living in Rochester."

"What are you doing there?"

"Going to school."

"Large school?"

"Very large."

"All boys?"

"All boys."

"And how do you stand?" said my mother.

"I'm the best boy in that school," I answered.

"Well," said my mother, with a return of her old fire, "I'd like to know what the other boys are like."

Now, one point in this story is the fact that my mother's mind went back to my school days, and remembered my little youthful self-prejudice when she'd forgotten everything else about me.

The other point is the moral. There's one there that you will find if you search for it.

Now, here's something else I remember. It's about the first time I ever stole a watermelon. "Stole" is a strong word. Stole? Stole? No, I don't mean that. It was the first time I ever withdrew a water-melon. It was the first time I ever extracted a watermelon. That is exactly the word I want—"extracted." It is definite. It is precise. It perfectly conveys my idea. Its use in dentistry connotes the delicate shade of meaning I am looking for. You know we never extract our own teeth.

And it was not my watermelon that I extracted. I extracted that wa-termelon from a farmer's wagon while he was inside negotiating with another customer. I carried that watermelon to one of the secluded recesses of the lumber-yard, and there I broke it open.

It was a green watermelon.

Well, do you know when I saw that I began to feel sorry—sorry—sorry. It seemed to me that I had done wrong. I reflected deeply. I reflected that I was young—I think I was just eleven. But I knew that though immature I did not lack moral advancement. I knew what a boy ought to do who had extracted a watermelon like that.

I considered George Washington, and what action he would have taken under similar circumstances. Then I knew there was just one thing to make me feel right inside, and that was—Restitution.

So I said to myself: "I will do that. I will take that green watermelon back where I got it from." And the minute I had said it I felt that great moral uplift that comes to you when you've made a noble resolution.

So I gathered up the biggest fragments, and I carried them back to the farmer's wagon, and I restored the watermelon—what was left of it. And I made him give me a good one in place of it, too.

And I told him he ought to be ashamed of himself going around working off his worthless, old, green watermelons on trusting purchasers who had to rely on him. How could they tell from the outside whether the melons were good or not? That was his business. And if he didn't reform, I told him I'd see that he didn't get any more of my trade—nor anybody else's I knew, if I could help it.

You know that man was as contrite as a revivalist's last convert. He said he was all broken up to think I'd gotten a green watermelon. He promised me he would never carry another green watermelon if he starved for it. And he drove off—a better man.

Now, do you see what I did for that man? He was on a downward path, and I rescued him. But all I got out of it was a watermelon.

Yet I'd rather have that memory—just that memory of the good I did for that depraved farmer—than all the material gain you can think of. Look at the lesson he got! I never got anything like that from it. But I ought to be satisfied. I was only eleven years old, but I secured everlasting benefit to other people.

The moral in this is perfectly clear, and I think there's one in the next memory I'm going to tell you about.

To go back to my childhood, there's another little incident that comes to me from which you can draw even another moral. It's about one of the times I went fishing. You see, in our house there was a sort of family prejudice against going fishing if you hadn't permission. But it would frequently be bad judgment to ask. So I went fishing secretly, as it were—way up the Mississippi. It was an exquisitely happy trip, I recall, with a very pleasant sensation.

Well, while I was away there was a tragedy in our town. A stranger, stopping over on his way East from California, was stabbed to death in an unseemly brawl.

Now, my father was justice of the peace, and because he was justice of the peace he was coroner; and since he was coroner he was also constable; and being constable he was sheriff; and out of consideration for his holding the office of sheriff he was likewise county clerk and a dozen other officials I don't think of just this minute.

I thought he had power of life or death; only he didn't use it over other boys. He was sort of an austere man. Somehow I didn't like being round him when I'd done anything he disapproved of. So that's the reason I wasn't often around.

Well, when this gentleman got knifed they communicated with the proper authority, the coroner, and they laid the corpse out in the coroner's office—our front sitting-room—in preparation for the inquest the next morning.

About nine or ten o'clock I got back from fishing. It was a little too late for me to be received by my folks, so I took my shoes off and slipped noiselessly up the back way to the sitting-room. I was very tired, and I didn't wish to disturb my people. So I groped my way to the sofa and lay down.

Now, I didn't know anything of what had happened during my absence. But I was sort of nervous on my own account—afraid of being caught, and rather dubious about the morning affair. And I had been lying there a few moments when my eyes gradually got used to the darkness, and I became aware of something on the other side of the room.

It was something foreign to the apartment. It had an uncanny appearance. And I sat up looking very hard, and wondering what in heaven this long, formless, vicious-looking thing might be.

First I thought I'd go and see. Then I thought, "Never mind that."

Mind you, I had no cowardly sensations whatever, but it didn't seem exactly prudent to investigate. But I somehow couldn't keep my eyes off the thing. And the more I looked at it the more disagreeably it grew on me. But I was resolved to play the man. So I decided to turn over and count a hundred, and let the patch of moonlight creep up and show me what the dickens it was.

Well, I turned over and tried to count, but I couldn't keep my mind on it. I kept thinking of that gruesome mass. I was losing count all the time, and going back and beginning over again. Oh no; I wasn't frightened—just annoyed. But by the time I'd gotten to the century mark I turned cautiously over and opened my eyes with great fortitude.

The moonlight revealed to me a marble-white human hand. Well, maybe I wasn't embarrassed! But then that changed to a creepy feeling again, and I thought I'd try the counting again. I don't know how many hours or weeks it was that I lay there counting hard. But the moonlight crept up that white arm, and it showed me a lead face and a terrible wound over the heart.

I could scarcely say that I was terror-stricken or anything like that. But somehow his eyes interested me so that I went right out of the window. I didn't need the sash. But it seemed easier to take it than leave it behind.

Now, let that teach you a lesson—I don't know just what it is. But at seventy years old I find that memory of peculiar value to me. I have been unconsciously guided by it all these years. Things that seemed pigeon-holed and remote are a perpetual influence. Yes, you're taught in so many ways. And you're so felicitously taught when you don't know it.

Here's something else that taught me a good deal.

When I was seventeen I was very bashful, and a sixteen-year-old girl came to stay a week with us. She was a peach, and I was seized with a happiness not of this world.

One evening my mother suggested that, to entertain her, I take I take her to the theater. I didn't really like to, because I was seventeen and sensitive about appearing in the streets with a girl. I couldn't see my way to enjoying my delight in public. But we went.

I didn't feel very happy. I couldn't seem to keep my mind on the play. I became unconscious after a while, that that was due less to my lovely company than my boots. They were sweet to look upon, as smooth as skin, but fitted ten times as close. I got oblivious to the play and the girl and the other people and everything but my boots until I hitched one partly off. The sensation was sensuously perfect. I couldn't help it. I had to get the other off, partly. Then I was obliged to get them off altogether, except that I kept my feet in the legs so they couldn't get away.

From that time I enjoyed the play. But the first thing I knew the curtain came down, like that, without my notice, and I hadn't any boots on. I tugged strenuously. And the people in our row got up and fussed and said things until the peach and I simply had to move on.

We moved—the girl on one arm and the boots under the other.

We walked home that way, sixteen blocks, with a retinue a mile long. Every time we passed a lamp-post death gripped me at the throat. But we got home—and I had on white socks.

If I live to be nine hundred and ninety-nine years old I don't suppose I could ever forget that walk. I remember it about as keenly as the chagrin I suffered on another occasion.

At one time in our domestic history we had a colored butler who had a failing. He could never remember to ask people who came to the door to state their business. So I used to buffer a good many calls unnecessarily.

One morning when I was especially busy he brought me a card engraved with a name I did not know. So I said, "What does he wish to see me for?" and Sylvester said, "Ah couldn't ask him, sah; he wuz a genlmun." "Return instantly," I thundered, "and inquire his mission. Ask him what's his game." Well, Sylvester returned with the announcement that he had lightning-rods to sell. "Indeed," said I, "things are coming to a fine pass when lightning-rod agents send up engraved cards." "He has pictures," added Sylvester. "Pictures, indeed! He may be peddling etchings. Has he a Russia leather case?" But Sylvester was too frightened to remember. I said, "I am going down to make it hot for that upstart!"

I went down the stairs, working up my temper all the way. When I got to the parlor I was in a fine frenzy concealed beneath a veneer of frigid courtesy. And when I looked in the door, sure enough he had a Russia leather case in his hand. But I didn't happen to notice that it was our Russia leather case.

And if you'd believe me, that man was sitting with a whole gallery of etchings spread out before him. But I didn't happen to notice that they were our etchings, spread out by some member of my family for some unguessed purpose.

Very curtly I asked the gentleman his business. With a surprised, timid manner he faltered that he had met my wife and daughter at Onteora, and they had asked him to call. Fine lie, I thought, and I froze him.

He seemed to be kind of nonplussed, and sat there fingering the etchings in the case until I told him he needn't bother, because we had those. That pleased him so much that he leaned over, in an embarrassed way, to pick up another from the floor. But I stopped him. I said, "We've got that, too." He seemed pitifully amazed, but I was congratulating myself on my great success.

Finally the gentleman asked where Mr. Winton lived; he'd met him in the mountains, too. So I said I'd show him gladly. And I did on the spot. And when he was gone I felt queer, because there were all his etchings spread out on the floor.

Well, my wife came in and asked me who had been in. I showed her the card, and told her all exultantly. To my dismay she nearly fainted. She told me he had been a most kind friend to them in the country, and had forgotten to tell me that he was expected our way. And she pushed me out of the door, and commanded me to get over to the Wintons in a hurry and get him back.

I came into the drawing-room, where Mrs. Winton was sitting up very stiff in a chair, beating me at my own game. Well, I began to put another light on things. Before many seconds Mrs. Winton saw it was time to change her temperature. In five minutes I had asked the man to luncheon, and she to dinner, and so on.

We made that fellow change his trip and stay a week, and we gave him the time of his life. Why, I don't believe we let him get sober the whole time.

I trust that you will carry away some good thought from these lessons I have given you, and that the memory of them will inspire you to higher things, and elevate you to plans far above the old—and—and—

And I tell you one thing, young ladies: I've had a better time with you today than with that peach fifty-three years ago.

WHEN IN DOUBT, TELL THE TRUTH

New York City, March 8, 1906

Mark Twain's speech at the dinner of the Freundschaft Society played off the words of introduction used by the dinner's toastmaster, Julius Frank, who referred to one of Pudd'nhead Wilson's sayings, "When in doubt, tell the truth." Wilson was the hero of a Twain novel and the maxim-maker for the travel book Following the Equator, *where this quotation first appeared.*

Mr. Chairman, Mr. Putzel, and Gentlemen of the Freundschaft,

That maxim I did invent, but never expected it to be applied to me. I did say, "When you are in doubt," but when I am in doubt myself I use more sagacity.

Mr. [Edward Marshall] Grout suggested that if I have anything to say against Mr. [Charles] Putzel, or any criticism of his career or his character, I am the last person to come out on account of that maxim and tell the truth. That is altogether a mistake.

I do think it is right for other people to be virtuous so that they can be happy hereafter, but if I knew every impropriety that even Mr. Putzel has committed in his life, I would not mention one of them. My judgment has been maturing for seventy years, and I have got to that point where I know better than that.

Mr. Putzel stands related to me in a very tender way (through the tax office), and it does not behoove me to say anything which could by any possibility militate against that condition of things.

Now, that word—taxes, taxes, taxes! I have heard it tonight. I have heard it all night. I wish somebody would change that subject; that is a very sore subject to me.

I was so relieved when Judge Leventritt did find something that was not taxable—when he said that the commissioner could not tax your patience. And that comforted me. We've got so much taxation. I don't know of a single foreign product that enters this country untaxed except the answer to prayer.

On an occasion like this the proprieties require that you merely pay compliments to the guest of the occasion, and I am merely here to pay compliments to the guest of the occasion, not to criticize him in any way, and I can say only complimentary things to him.

When I went down to the tax office some time ago, for the first time in New York, I saw Mr. Putzel sitting in the "Seat of Perjury." I recognized him right away. I warmed to him on the spot. I didn't know that I had ever seen him before, but just as soon as I saw him I recognized him. I had met him twenty-five years before, and at that time had achieved a knowledge of his abilities and something more than that.

I thought: "Now, this is the man whom I saw twenty-five years ago." On that occasion I not only went free at his hands, but carried off something more than that. I hoped it would happen again.

It was twenty-five years ago when I saw a young clerk in Putnam's bookstore. I went in there and asked for George Haven Putnam, and handed him my card, and then the young man said Mr. Putnam was busy and I couldn't see him. Well, I had merely called in a social way, and so it didn't matter.

I was going out when I saw a great big, fat, interesting-looking book lying there, and I took it up. It was an account of the invasion of England in the fourteenth century by the Preaching Friar, and it interested me.

I asked him the price of it, and he said four dollars.

"Well," I said, "what discount do you allow to publishers?"

He said: "Forty percent off."

I said: "All right, I am a publisher."

He put down the figure, forty percent off, on a card.

Then I said: "What discount do you allow to authors?"

He said: "Forty percent off."

"Well," I said, "set me down as an author."

"Now," said I, "what discount do you allow to the clergy?"

He said: "Forty percent off."

I said to him that I was only on the road, and that I was studying for the ministry. I asked him wouldn't he knock off twenty percent for that. He set down the figure, and he never smiled once.

I was working off these humorous brilliancies on him and getting no return—not a scintillation in his eye, not a spark of recognition of what I was doing there. I was almost in despair.

I thought I might try him once more, so I said: "Now, I am also a member of the human race. Will you let me have the ten percent off for that?" He set it down, and never smiled.

Well, I gave it up. I said: "There is my card with my address on it, but I have not any money with me. Will you please send the bill to Hartford?" I took up the book and was going away.

He said: "Wait a minute. There is forty cents coming to you."

When I met him in the tax office I thought maybe I could make something again, but I could not. But I had not any idea I could when I came, and as it turned out I did get off entirely free.

I put up my hand and made a statement. It gave me a good deal of pain to do that. I was not used to it. I was born and reared in the higher circles of Missouri, and there we don't do such things—didn't in my time, but we have got that little matter settled—got a sort of tax levied on me.

Then he touched me. Yes, he touched me this time, because he cried—cried! He was moved to tears to see that I, a virtuous person only a year before, after immersion for one year—during one year in the New York morals—had no more conscience than a millionaire.

IN AID OF THE BLIND

New York City, March 29, 1906

To raise money for the New York State Association for Promoting the Interests of the Blind, Twain presided over a public meeting at the Waldorf-Astoria.

If you detect any awkwardness in my movements and infelicities in my conduct I will offer the explanation that I never presided at a meeting of any kind before in my life, and that I do find it out of my line. I supposed I could do anything anybody else could, but I recognize that experience helps, and I do feel the lack of that experience. I don't feel as graceful and easy as I ought to be in order to impress an audience. I shall not pretend that I know how to umpire a meeting like this, and I shall just take the humble place of the Essex band.

There was a great gathering in a small New England town about twenty-five years ago. I remember that circumstance because there was something that happened at that time. It was a great occasion. They gathered in the militia and orators and everybody from all the towns around. It was an extraordinary occasion.

The little local paper threw itself into ecstasies of admiration and tried to do itself proud from beginning to end. It praised the orators, the militia, and all the bands that came from everywhere, and all this in honest country newspaper detail, but the writer ran out of adjectives toward the end. Having exhausted his whole magazine of praise and glorification, he found he still had one band left over. He had to say something about it, and he said: "The Essex band done the best it could."

I am an Essex band on this occasion, and I am going to get through as well as inexperience and good intentions will enable me. I have got all the documents here necessary to instruct you in the objects and intentions of this meeting and also of the association which has called the meeting. But they are too voluminous. I could not pack those statistics into my head, and I had to give it up. I shall have to just reduce all that mass of statistics to a few salient facts. There are too many statistics and figures for me. I never could do anything with figures, never had any talent for mathematics, never accomplished anything in my efforts at that rugged study, and today the only mathematics I know is multiplication, and the minute I get away up in that, as soon as I reach nine times seven— . . .

I've got it now. It's eighty-four. Well, I can get that far all right with a little hesitation. After that I am uncertain, and I can't manage a statistic.

This association for the— . . .

Oh yes, for promoting the interests of the blind. It's a long name. If I could I would write it out for you and let you take it home and study it, but I don't know how to spell it. And Mr. Carnegie is down in Virginia somewhere. Well, anyway, the object of that association which has been recently organized, five months ago, in fact, is in the hands of very, very energetic, intelligent, and capable people, and they will push it to success very surely, and all the more surely if you will give them a little of your assistance out of your pockets.

The intention, the purpose, is to search out all the blind and find work for them to do so that they may earn their own bread. Now it is dismal enough to be blind—it is dreary, dreary life at best, but it can be largely ameliorated by finding something for these poor blind people to do with their hands. The time passes so heavily that it is never day or night with them, it is always night, and when they have to sit with folded hands and with nothing to do to amuse or entertain or employ their minds, it is drearier and drearier.

And then the knowledge they have that they must subsist on charity, and so often reluctant charity, it would renew their lives if they could have something to do with their hands and pass their time and at the same time earn their bread, and know the sweetness of the bread which is the result of the labor of one's own hands. They need that cheer and pleasure. It is the only way you can turn their night into day, to give them happy hearts, the only thing you can put in the place of the blessed sun. That you can do in the way I speak of.

Blind people generally who have seen the light know what it is to miss the light. Those who have gone blind since they were twenty years old—their lives are unendingly dreary. But they can be taught to use their hands and to employ themselves at a great many industries. That association from which this draws its birth in Cambridge, Massachusetts, has taught its blind to make many things. They make them better than most people, and more honest than people who have the use of their eyes. The goods they make are readily salable. People like them. And so they are supporting themselves, and it is a matter of cheer, cheer. They pass their time now not too irksomely as they formerly did.

What this association needs and wants is $15,000. The figures are set down, and what the money is for, and there is no graft in it or I would not be here. And they hope to beguile that out of your pockets, and you will find affixed to the program an opportunity, that little blank which you will fill out and promise so much money now or tomorrow or some time. Then, there is another opportunity which is still better, and that is that you shall subscribe an annual sum.

I have invented a good many useful things in my time, but never anything better than that of getting money out of people who don't want to part with it. It is always for good objects, of course. This is the plan: When you call upon a person to contribute to a great and good object, and you think he should furnish about $1,000, he disappoints you as like as not. Much the best way to work him to supply that thousand dollars is to split it into parts and contribute, say a hundred dollars a year, or fifty, or whatever the sum may be. Let him contribute ten or twenty a year. He doesn't feel that, but he does feel it when you call upon him to contribute a large amount. When you get used to it you would rather contribute than borrow money.

I tried it in Helen Keller's case. Mr. Hutton wrote me in 1896 or 1897 when I was in London and said: "The gentleman who has been so liberal in taking care of Helen Keller has died without making provision for her in his will, and now they don't know what to do." They were proposing to raise a fund, and he thought $50,000 enough to furnish an income of $2,400 or $2,500 a year for the support of that wonderful girl and her wonderful teacher, Miss Sullivan, now Mrs. Macy.

I wrote to Mr. Hutton and said: "Go on, get up your fund. It will be slow, but if you want quick work, I propose this system," the system I speak of, of asking people to contribute such and such a sum from year to year and drop out whenever they please, and he would find there wouldn't be any difficulty, people wouldn't feel the burden of it. And he wrote back saying he had raised the $2,400 a year indefinitely by that system in a single afternoon. We would like to do something just like that tonight. We will take as many checks as you care to give. You can leave your donations in the big room outside.

I knew once what it was to be blind. I shall never forget that experience. I have been as blind as anybody ever was for three or four hours, and the sufferings that I endured and the mishaps and the accidents that are burning in my memory make my sympathy rise when I feel for the blind and always shall feel.

I once went to Heidelberg on an excursion. I took a clergyman along with me, the Rev. Joseph Twichell, of Hartford, who is still among the living despite that fact. I always travel with clergymen when I can. It is better for them, it is better for me. And any preacher who goes out with me in stormy weather and without a lightning rod is a good one. The Reverend Twichell is one of those people filled with patience and endurance, two good ingredients for a man traveling with me, so we got along very well together. In that old town they have not altered a house nor built one in 1,500 years. We went to the inn and they placed Twichell and me in a most colossal bedroom, the largest I ever saw or heard of. It was as big as this room.

I didn't take much notice of the place. I didn't really get my bearings. I noticed Twichell got a German bed about two feet wide, the kind in which you've got to lie on your edge, because there isn't room to lie on your back, and he was way down south in that big room, and I was way up north at the other end of it, with a regular Sahara in between.

We went to bed. Twichell went to sleep, but then he had his conscience loaded and it was easy for him to get to sleep. I couldn't get to sleep. It was one of those torturing kinds of lovely summer nights when you hear various kinds of noises now and then. A mouse away off in the southwest. You throw things at the mouse. That encourages the mouse. But I couldn't stand it, and about two o'clock I got up and thought I would give it up and go out in the square where there was one of those tinkling fountains, and sit on its brink and dream, full of romance.

I got out of bed, and I ought to have lit a candle, but I didn't think of it until it was too late. It was the darkest place that ever was. There has never been darkness any thicker than that. It just lay in cakes.

I thought that before dressing I would accumulate my clothes. I pawed around in the dark and found everything packed together on the floor except one sock. I couldn't get on the track of that sock. It might have occurred to me that maybe it was in the wash. But I didn't think of that. I went excursioning on my hands and knees. Presently I thought, "I am never going to find it; I'll go back to bed again." That is what I tried to do during the next three hours. I had lost the bearings of that bed. I was going in the wrong direction all the time. By-and-by I came in collision with a chair and that encouraged me.

It seemed to me, as far as I could recollect, there was only a chair here and there and yonder, five or six of them scattered over this territory, and I thought maybe after I found that chair I might find the next one. Well, I did. And I found another and another and another. I kept going around on my hands and knees, having those sudden collisions, and finally when I banged into another chair I almost lost my temper. And I raised up, garbed as I was, not for public exhibition, right in front of a mirror fifteen or sixteen feet high.

I hadn't noticed the mirror; didn't know it was there. And when I saw myself in the mirror I was frightened out of my wits. I don't allow any ghosts to bite me, and I took up a chair and smashed at it. A million pieces. Then I reflected. That's the way I always do, and it's unprofitable unless a man has had much experience that way and has clear judgment. And I had judgment, and I would have had to pay for that mirror if I hadn't recollected to say it was Twichell who broke it.

Then I got down on my hands and knees and went on another exploring expedition.

As far as I could remember there were six chairs in that Oklahoma, and one table, a great big heavy table, not a good table to hit with your head when rushing madly along. In the course of time I collided with thirty-five chairs and tables enough to stock that dining-room out there. It was a hospital for decayed furniture, and it was in a worse condition when I got through with it. I went on and on, and at last got to a place where I could feel my way up, and there was a shelf. I knew that wasn't in the middle of the room. Up to that time I was afraid I had gotten out of the city.

I was very careful and pawed along that shelf, and there was a pitcher of water about a foot high, and it was at the head of Twichell's bed, but I didn't know it. I felt that pitcher going and I grabbed at it, but it didn't help any and came right down in Twichell's face and nearly drowned him. But it woke him up. I was grateful to have company on any terms. He lit a match, and there I was, way down south when I ought to have been back up yonder. My bed was out of sight it was so far away. You needed a telescope to find it. Twichell comforted me and I scrubbed him off and we got sociable.

But that night wasn't wasted. I had my pedometer on my leg. Twichell and I were in a pedometer match. Twichell had longer legs than I. The only way I could keep up was to wear my pedometer to bed. I always walk in my sleep, and on this occasion I gained sixteen miles on him. After all, I never found that sock. I never have seen it from that day to this. But that adventure taught me what it is to be blind. That was one of the most serious occasions of my whole life, yet I never can speak of it without somebody thinking it isn't serious. You try it and see how serious it is to be as the blind are and I was that night. . . .

It is now my privilege to present to you Mr. [Joseph] Choate. I don't have to really introduce him. I don't have to praise him, or to flatter him. I could say truly that in the forty-seven years I have been familiarly acquainted with him he has always been the handsomest man America has ever produced. And I hope and believe he will hold the belt forty-five years more. He has served his country ably, faithfully, and brilliantly. He stands at the summit, at the very top in the esteem and regard of his countrymen, and if I could say one word which would lift him any higher in his countrymen's esteem and affection, I would say that word whether it was true or not.

THE ROBERT FULTON FUND

New York City, April 19, 1906

Frederick D. Grant, the son of the former president Ulysses S. Grant, offered Twain money to speak at the Robert Fulton Monument Association Benefit, an organization Twain supported. For his speech at Carnegie Hall, Twain turned down the money, writing, "I shall be glad to do it, but I must stipulate that you keep the $1,000, and add it to the Memorial Fund as my contribution to erect a monument in New York to the memory of the man who applied steam to navigation." Twain, calling for donations to support the victims of April 18th's earthquake and fire in San Francisco, formally announced at this benefit that "This is my last appearance on the paid platform. I shall not retire from the gratis platform until I am buried, and courtesy will compel me to keep still and not disturb the others. Now, since I must, I shall say good-bye. I see many faces in this audience well known to me. They are all my friends, and I feel that those I don't know are my friends, too. I wish to consider that you represent the nation, and that in saying good-bye to you I am saying good-bye to the nation. In the great name of humanity, let me say this final word: I offer an appeal in behalf of that vast, pathetic multitude of fathers, mothers, and helpless little children. They were sheltered and happy two days ago. Now they are wandering, forlorn, hopeless, and homeless, the victims of a great disaster. So I beg of you, I beg of you, to open your hearts and open your purses and remember San Francisco, the smitten city."

I wish to deliver a historical address. I've been studying the history of—er—a—let me see—a *[then he stopped in confusion, and walked over to Gen. Fred D. Grant, who sat at the head of the platform. He leaned over in a whisper, and then returned to the front of the stage and continued]*. Oh yes! I've been studying Robert Fulton. I've been studying a biographical sketch of Robert Fulton, the inventor of—er—a—let's see—oh yes, the inventor of the electric telegraph and the Morse sewing-machine. Also, I understand he invented the air—diria—pshaw! I have it at last—the dirigible balloon. Yes, the dirigible but it is a difficult word, and I don't see why anybody should marry a couple of words like that when

128

they don't want to be married at all and are likely to quarrel with each other all the time. I should put that couple of words under the ban of the United States Supreme Court, under its decision of a few days ago, and take 'em out and drown 'em.

I used to know Fulton. It used to do me good to see him dashing through the town on a wild broncho.

And Fulton was born in er—a—well, it doesn't make much difference where he was born, does it? I remember a man who came to interview me once, to get a sketch of my life. I consulted with a friend—a practical man—before he came, to know how I should treat him.

"Whenever you give the interviewer a fact," he said, "give him another fact that will contradict it. Then he'll go away with a jumble that he can't use at all. Be gentle, be sweet, smile like an idiot—just be natural." That's what my friend told me to do, and I did it.

"Where were you born?" asked the interviewer.

"Well—er—a," I began, "I was born in Alabama, or Alaska, or the Sandwich Islands; I don't know where, but right around there somewhere. And you had better put it down before you forget it."

"But you weren't born in all those places," he said.

"Well, I've offered you three places. Take your choice. They're all at the same price."

"How old are you?" he asked.

"I shall be nineteen in June," I said.

"Why, there's such a discrepancy between your age and your looks," he said.

"Oh, that's nothing," I said, "I was born discrepantly."

Then we got to talking about my brother Samuel, and he told me my explanations were confusing.

"I suppose he is dead," I said. "Some said that he was dead and some said that he wasn't."

"Did you bury him without knowing whether he was dead or not?" asked the reporter.

"There was a mystery," said I. "We were twins, and one day when we were two weeks old—that is, he was one week old, and I was one week old—we got mixed up in the bathtub, and one of us drowned. We never could tell which. One of us had a strawberry birthmark on the back of his hand. There it is on my hand. This is the one that was drowned. There's no doubt about it."

"Where's the mystery?" he said.

"Why, don't you see how stupid it was to bury the wrong twin?" I answered. I didn't explain it any more because he said the explanation confused him. To me it is perfectly plain.

But, to get back to Fulton. I'm going along like an old man I used to know who used to start to tell a story about his grandfather. He had an awfully retentive memory, and he never finished the story, because he switched off into something else. He used to tell about how his grandfather one day went into a pasture, where there was a ram. The old man dropped a silver dime in the grass, and stooped over to pick it up. The ram was observing him, and took the old man's action as an invitation.

Just as he was going to finish about the ram this friend of mine would recall that his grandfather had a niece who had a glass eye. She used to loan that glass eye to another lady friend, who used it when she received company. The eye didn't fit the friend's face, and it was loose. And whenever she winked it would turn over.

Then he got on the subject of accidents, and he would tell a story about how he believed accidents never happened.

"There was an Irishman coming down a ladder with a hod of bricks," he said, "and a Dutchman was standing on the ground below. The Irishman fell on the Dutchman and killed him. Accident? Never! If the Dutchman hadn't been there the Irishman would have been killed. Why didn't the Irishman fall on a dog which was next to the Dutchman? Because the dog would have seen him coming."

Then he'd get off from the Dutchman to an uncle named Reginald Wilson. Reginald went into a carpet factory one day, and got twisted into the machinery's belt. He went excursioning around the factory until he was properly distributed and was woven into sixty-nine yards of the best three-ply carpet. His wife bought the carpet, and then she erected a monument to his memory. It read:

> Sacred to the memory
> of
> sixty-nine yards of the best three-ply carpet
> containing the mortal remainders of
>
> REGINALD WILSON
>
> Go thou and do likewise

And so on he would ramble about telling the story of his grandfather until we never were told whether he found the ten-cent piece or whether something else happened.

BILLIARDS

New York City, April 24, 1906

At a billiards benefit at Madison Square Garden for the victims of the San Francisco earthquake and fire, Twain spoke and told a story.

The game of billiards has destroyed my naturally sweet disposition. Once, when I was an underpaid reporter in Virginia City, whenever I wished to play billiards I went out to look for an easy mark. One day a stranger came to town and opened a billiard parlor. I looked him over casually. When he proposed a game, I answered, "All right."

"Just knock the balls around a little so that I can get your gait," he said; and when I had done so, he remarked: "I will be perfectly fair with you. I'll play you left-handed." I felt hurt, for he was cross-eyed, freckled, and had red hair, and I determined to teach him a lesson. He won first shot, ran out, took my half-dollar, and all I got was the opportunity to chalk my cue.

"If you can play like that with your left hand," I said, "I'd like to see you play with your right."

"I can't, he said. "I'm left-handed."

131

SPELLING AND PICTURES

New York City, September 19, 1906

Twain addressed the Associated Press, about 150 members, at the Waldorf-Astoria at its annual dinner.

I am here to make an appeal to the nations in behalf of the simplified spelling. I have come here because they cannot all be reached except through you. There are only two forces that can carry light to all the corners of the globe—only two—the sun in the heavens and the Associated Press down here. I may seem to be flattering the sun, but I do not mean it so; I am meaning only to be just and fair all around. You speak with a million voices; no one can reach so many races, so many hearts and intellects, as you—except Rudyard Kipling, and he cannot do it without your help. If the Associated Press will adopt and use our simplified forms, and thus spread them to the ends of the earth, covering the whole spacious planet with them as with a garden of flowers, our difficulties are at an end.

Every day of the three hundred and sixty-five the only pages of the world's countless newspapers that are read by all the human beings and angels and devils that can read, are these pages that are built out of Associated Press dispatches. And so I beg you, I beseech you—oh, I implore you to spell them in our simplified forms. Do this daily, constantly, persistently, for three months—only three months—it is all I ask. The infallible result?—victory, victory all down the line. For by that time all eyes here and above and below will have become adjusted to the change and in love with it, and the present clumsy and ragged forms will be grotesque to the eye and revolting to the soul. And we shall be rid of phthisis and phthisic and pneumonia and pneumatics, and diphtheria and pterodactyl, and all those other insane words which no man addicted to the simple Christian life can try to spell and not lose some of the bloom of his piety in the demoralizing attempt. Do not doubt it. We are chameleons, and our partialities and prejudices change places with an easy and blessed facility, and we are soon wonted

132

to the change and happy in it. We do not regret our old, yellow fangs and snags and tushes after we have worn nice, fresh, uniform store teeth a while.

Do I seem to be seeking the good of the world? That is the idea. It is my public attitude; privately I am merely seeking my own profit. We all do it, but it is sound and it is virtuous, for no public interest is anything other or nobler than a massed accumulation of private interests. In 1883, when the simplified-spelling movement first tried to make a noise, I was indifferent to it; more—I even irreverently scoffed at it. What I needed was an object-lesson, you see. It is the only way to teach some people. Very well, I got it. At that time I was scrambling along, earning the family's bread on magazine work at seven cents a word, compound words at single rates, just as it is in the dark present. I was the property of a magazine, a seven-cent slave under a boiler-iron contract. One day there came a note from the editor requiring me to write ten pages on this revolting text: "Considerations concerning the alleged subterranean holophotal extemporaneousness of the conchyliaceous superimbrication of the Ornithorhyncus, as foreshadowed by the unintelligibility of its plesiosaurian anisodactylous aspects."

Ten pages of that. Each and every word a seventeen-jointed vestibuled railroad train. Seven cents a word. I saw starvation staring the family in the face. I went to the editor, and I took a stenographer along so as to have the interview down in black and white, for no magazine editor can ever remember any part of a business talk except the part that's got graft in it for him and the magazine. I said, "Read that text, Jackson, and let it go on the record; read it out loud." He read it: "Considerations concerning the alleged subterranean holophotal extemporaneousness of the conchyliaceous superimbrication of the Ornithorhyncus, as foreshadowed by the unintelligibility of its plesiosaurian anisodactylous aspects."

I said, "You want ten pages of those rumbling, great, long, summer thunderpeals, and you expect to get them at seven cents a peal?"

He said, "A word's a word, and seven cents is the contract; what are you going to do about it?" I said, "Jackson, this is cold-blooded oppression. What's an average English word?"

He said, "Six letters."

I said, "Nothing of the kind; that's French, and includes the spaces between the words; an average English word is four letters and a half. By hard, honest labor I've dug all the large words out of my vocabulary and shaved it down till the average is three letters and a half. I can put one thousand and two hundred words on your page, and there's not another man alive that can come within two hundred of it. My page is worth eighty-four dollars to me. It takes exactly as long to fill your magazine page with long words as it does with short ones—four hours. Now, then, look at the criminal injustice of this requirement of yours. I am careful, I am economical of my time and labor. For the family's sake I've got to be so. So I never write 'metropolis' for seven cents, because I can get the same money for 'city.' I never write 'policeman,' because I can get the same price for 'cop.' And so on and so on. I never write 'valetudinarian' at all, for not even hunger and wretchedness can humble me to the point where I will do a word like that for seven cents; I wouldn't do it for fifteen. Examine your obscene text, please, count the words."

He counted and said it was twenty-four. I asked him to count the letters. He made it two hundred and three.

I said, "Now, I hope you see the whole size of your crime. With my vocabulary I would make sixty words out of those two hundred and five letters, and get four dollars and twenty cents for it; whereas for your inhuman twenty-four I would get only one dollar and sixty-eight cents. Ten pages of these sky-scrapers of yours would pay me only about three hundred dollars; in my simplified vocabulary the same space and the same labor would pay me eight hundred and forty dollars. I do not wish to work upon this scandalous job by the piece. I want to be hired by the year." He coldly refused.

I said: "Then for the sake of the family, if you have no feeling for me, you ought at least to allow me overtime on that word extemporaneousness." Again he coldly refused. I seldom say a harsh word to any one, but I was not master of myself then, and I spoke right out and called him an anisodactylous plesiosaurian conchyliaceous Ornithorhyneus, and rotten to the heart with holophotal subterranean extemporaneousness. God forgive me for that wanton crime; he lived only two hours.

From that day to this I have been a devoted and hard-working member of the heaven-born institution, the International Association for the Prevention of Cruelty to Authors, and now I am laboring with Carnegie's Simplified Committee, and with my heart in the work.

Now then, let us look at this mighty question reasonably, rationally, sanely—yes, and calmly, not excitedly. What is the real function, the essential function, the supreme function, of language? Isn't it merely to convey ideas and emotions? Certainly. Then if we can do it with words of phonetic brevity and compactness, why keep the present cumbersome forms? But can we? Yes. I hold in my hand the proof of it. Here is a letter written by a woman, right out of her heart of hearts. I think she never saw a spelling-book in her life. The spelling is her own. There isn't a waste letter in it anywhere. It reduces the phonetics to the last gasp—it squeezes the surplusage out of every word—there's no spelling that can begin with it on this planet outside of the White

House. And as for the punctuation, there isn't any. It is all one sentence, eagerly and breathlessly uttered, without break or pause in it anywhere. The letter is absolutely genuine—I have the proofs of that in my possession. I can't stop to spell the words for you, but you can take the letter presently and comfort your eyes with it. I will read the letter:

> Miss—— dear freind I took some Close into the armerry and give them to you to Send too the suffrers out to California and i Hate to truble you but i got to have one of them Back it was a black oll wolle Shevyott With a jacket to Mach trimed Kind of Fancy no 38 Burst measure and passy menterry acrost the front And the color i woodent Trubble you but it belonged to my brothers wife and she is Mad about it i thoght she was willin but she want she says she want done with it and she was going to Wear it a Spell longer she ant so free harted as what i am and she Has got more to do with Than i have having a Husband to Work and slave For her i gess you remember Me I am shot and stout and light complected i torked with you quite a spell about the suffrars and said it was orful about that erth quake I shoodent wondar if they had another one rite off seeine general Condision of the country is Kind of Explossive i hate to take that Black dress away from the suffrars but i will hunt round And see if i can get another One if i can i will call to the armerry for it if you will jest lay it asside so no more at present from your True freind
>
> i liked your
> appearance very Much

Now you see what simplified spelling can do.

It can convey any fact you need to convey; and it can pour out emotions like a sewer. I beg you, I beseech you, to adopt our spelling, and print all your dispatches in it.

Now I wish to say just one entirely serious word: I have reached a time of life, seventy years and a half, where none of the concerns of this world have much interest for me personally. I think I can speak dispassionately upon this matter, because in the little while that I have got to remain here I can get along very well with these old-fashioned forms, and I don't propose to make any trouble about it at all. I shall soon be where they won't care how I spell so long as I keep the Sabbath.

There are eighty-two millions of us people that use this orthography, and it ought to be simplified in our behalf, but it is kept in its present condition to satisfy one million people who like to have their literature in the old form. That looks to me to be rather selfish, and we keep the forms as they are while we have got one million people coming in here from foreign countries every year and they have got to struggle with this orthography of ours, and it keeps them back and damages their citizenship for years until they learn to spell the language, if they ever do learn. This is merely sentimental argument.

People say it is the spelling of Chaucer and Spenser and Shakespeare and a lot of other people who do not know how to spell anyway, and it has been transmitted to us and we preserved it and wish to preserve it because of its ancient and hallowed associations.

Now, I don't see that there is any real argument about that. If that argument is good, then it would be a good argument not to banish the flies and the cockroaches from hospitals because they have been there so long that the patients have got used to them and they feel a tenderness for them on account of the associations. Why, it is like preserving a cancer in a family because it is a family cancer, and we are bound to it by the test of affection and reverence and old, moldy antiquity.

I think that this declaration to improve this orthography of ours is our family cancer, and I wish we could reconcile ourselves to have it cut out and let the family cancer go.

Now, you see before you the wreck and ruin of what was once a young person like yourselves. I am exhausted by the heat of the day. I must take what is left of this wreck and run out of your presence and carry it away to my home and spread it out there and sleep the sleep of the righteous. There is nothing much left of me but my age and my righteousness, but I leave with you my love and my blessing, and may you always keep your youth.

MY FIRST APPEARANCE

Norfolk, Connecticut, September 22, 1906

Following a musical recital by his daughter Clara Clemens, who was making her debut as a contralto, Twain spoke to the audience about stage-fright.

My heart goes out in sympathy to any one who is making his first appearance before an audience of human beings. By a direct process of memory I go back forty years, less one month—for I'm older than I look.

I recall the occasion of my first appearance. San Francisco knew me then only as a reporter, and I was to make my bow to San Francisco as a lecturer. I knew that nothing short of compulsion would get me to the theater. So I bound myself by a hard-and-fast contract so that I could not escape. I got to the theater forty-five minutes before the hour set for the lecture. My knees were shaking so that I didn't know whether I could stand up. If there is an awful, horrible malady in the world, it is stage-fright—and sea-sickness. They are a pair. I had stage-fright then for the first and last time. I was only seasick once, too. It was on a little ship on which there were two hundred other passengers. *I-was-sick.* I was so sick that there wasn't any left for those other two hundred passengers.

It was dark and lonely behind the scenes in that theater, and I peeked through the little peek-holes they have in theater curtains and looked into the big auditorium. That was dark and empty, too. By-and-by it lighted up, and the audience began to arrive.

I had got a number of friends of mine, stalwart men, to sprinkle themselves through the audience armed with big clubs. Every time I said anything they could possibly guess I intended to be funny they were to pound those clubs on the floor. Then there was a kind lady in a box up there, also a good friend of mine, the wife of the governor. She was to watch me intently, and whenever I glanced toward her she was going to deliver a gubernatorial laugh that would lead the whole audience into applause.

At last I began. I had the manuscript tucked under a United States flag in front of me where I could get at it in case of need. But I managed to get started without it. I walked up and down—I was young in those days and needed the exercise—and talked and talked.

Right in the middle of the speech I had placed a gem. I had put in a moving, pathetic part which was to get at the hearts and souls of my hearers. When I delivered it they did just what I hoped and expected. They sat silent and awed. I had touched them. Then I happened to glance up at the box where the Governor's wife was—you know what happened.

Well, after the first agonizing five minutes, my stage-fright left me, never to return. I know if I was going to be hanged I could get up and make a good showing, and I intend to. But I shall never forget my feelings before the agony left me, and I got up here to thank you for her for helping my daughter, by your kindness, to live through her first appearance. And I want to thank you for your appreciation of her singing, which is, by-the-way, hereditary.

DRESS REFORM AND COPYRIGHT

Washington, D.C., December 7, 1906

While a copyright law was under discussion, Twain went to Washington to appear before the Congressional committee in charge of it. He gave this speech to reporters, which never touches on copyright, while waiting to be called before the committee. His speech to the committee follows in the next section.

Why don't you ask why I am wearing such apparently unseasonable clothes? I'll tell you. I have found that when a man reaches the advanced age of seventy-one years, as I have, the continual sight of dark clothing is likely to have a depressing effect upon him. Light-colored clothing is more pleasing to the eye and enlivens the spirit. Now, of course, I cannot compel every one to wear such clothing just for my especial benefit, so I do the next best thing and wear it myself.

Of course, before a man reaches my years the fear of criticism might prevent him from indulging his fancy. I am not afraid of that. I am decidedly for pleasing color combinations in dress. I like to see the women's clothes, say, at the opera. What can be more depressing than the somber black which custom requires men to wear upon state occasions? A group of men in evening clothes looks like a flock of crows, and is just about as inspiring.

After all, what is the purpose of clothing? Are not clothes intended primarily to preserve dignity and also to afford comfort to their wearer? Now I know of nothing more uncomfortable than the present-day clothes of men. The finest clothing made is a person's own skin, but, of course, society demands something more than this.

The best-dressed man I have ever seen, however, was a native of the Sandwich Islands who attracted my attention thirty years ago. Now, when that man wanted to don especial dress to honor a public occasion or a holiday, why, he occasionally put on a pair of spectacles. Otherwise the clothing with which God had provided him sufficed.

Of course, I have ideas of dress reform. For one thing, why not adopt some of the women's styles? Goodness knows, they adopt enough of ours. Take the peek-a-boo waist, for instance. It has the obvious advantages of being cool and comfortable, and in addition it is almost always made up in pleasing colors which cheer and do not depress.

It is true that I dressed the Connecticut Yankee at King Arthur's Court in a plug-hat, but, let's see, that was twenty-five years ago. Then no man was considered fully dressed until he donned a plug-hat. Nowadays I think that no man is dressed until he leaves it home. Why, when I left home yesterday they trotted out a plug-hat for me to wear.

"You must wear it," they told me; "why, just think of going to Washington without a plug-hat!" But I said no; I would wear a derby or nothing. Why, I believe I could walk along the streets of New York—I never do—but still I think I could—and I should never see a well-dressed man wearing a plug-hat. If I did I should suspect him of something. I don't know just what, but I would suspect him.

Why, when I got up on the second story of that Pennsylvania ferry-boat coming down here yesterday I saw Howells coming along. He was the only man on the boat with a plug-hat, and I tell you he felt ashamed of himself. He said he had been persuaded to wear it against his better sense. But just think of a man nearly seventy years old who has not a mind of his own on such matters!

(*"Are you doing any work now?" the youngest and most serious reporter asked.*)

Work? I retired from work on my seventieth birthday. Since then I have been putting in merely twenty-six hours a day dictating my autobiography, which, as John Phoenix said in regard to his autograph, may be relied upon as authentic, as it is written exclusively by me. But it is not to be published in full until I am thoroughly dead. I have made it as caustic, fiendish, and devilish as possible. It will fill many volumes, and I shall continue writing it until the time comes for me to join the angels. It is going to be a terrible autobiography. It will make the hair of some folks curl. But it cannot be published until I am dead, and the persons mentioned in it and their children and grandchildren are dead. It is something awful!

(*"Can you tell us the names of some of the notables that are here to see you off?"*)

I don't know. I am so shy. My shyness takes a peculiar phase. I never look a person in the face. The reason is that I am afraid they may know me and that I may not know them, which makes it very embarrassing for both of us. I always wait for the other person to speak. I know lots of people, but I don't know who they are. It is all a matter of ability to observe things. I never observe anything now. I gave up the habit years ago. You should keep a habit up if you want to become proficient in it. For instance, I was a pilot once, but I gave it up, and I do not believe the captain of the *Minneapolis* would let me navigate his ship to London. Still, if I think that he is not on the job I may go up on the bridge and offer him a few suggestions.

AMERICAN COPYRIGHT

Washington, D.C., December 7, 1906

With other authors, Twain appeared before the Congressional Committee on Patents about the new Copyright Bill.

I have read this bill. At least I have read such portions as I could understand. Nobody but a practiced legislator can read the bill and thoroughly understand it, and I am not a practiced legislator.

I am interested particularly and especially in the part of the bill which concerns my trade. I like that extension of copyright life to the author's life and fifty years afterward. I think that would satisfy any reasonable author, because it would take care of his children. Let the grandchildren take care of themselves. That would take care of my daughters, and after that I am not particular. I shall then have long been out of this struggle, independent of it, indifferent to it.

It isn't objectionable to me that all the trades and professions in the United States are protected by the bill. I like that. They are all important and worthy, and if we can take care of them under the copyright law I should like to see it done. I should like to see oyster culture added, and anything else.

I am aware that copyright must have a limit, because that is required by the Constitution of the United States, which sets aside the earlier Constitution, which we call the decalogue. The decalogue says you shall not take away from any man his profit. I don't like to be obliged to use the harsh term. What the decalogue really says is, "Thou shalt not steal," but I am trying to use more polite language.

The laws of England and America do take it away, do select but one class, the people who create the literature of the land. They always talk handsomely about the literature of the land, always what a fine, great, monumental thing a great literature is, and in the midst of their enthusiasm they turn around and do what they can to discourage it.

I know we must have a limit, but forty-two years is too much of a limit. I am quite unable to guess why there should be a limit at all to the possession of the product of a man's labor. There is no limit to real estate.

Doctor Hale has suggested that a man might just as well, after discovering a coal-mine and working it forty-two years, have the government step in and take it away.

What is the excuse? It is that the author who produced that book has had the profit of it long enough, and therefore the government takes a profit which does not belong to it and generously gives it to the 88,000,000 of people. But it doesn't do anything of the kind. It merely takes the author's property, takes his children's bread, and gives the publisher double profit. He goes on publishing the book and as many of his confederates as choose to go into the conspiracy do so, and they rear families in affluence.

And they continue the enjoyment of those ill-gotten gains generation after generation forever, for they never die. In a few weeks or months or years I shall be out of it, I hope under a monument. I hope I shall not be entirely forgotten, and I shall subscribe to the monument myself. But I shall not be caring what happens if there are fifty years left of my copyright. My copyright produces annually a good deal more than I can use, but my children can use it. I can get along; I know a lot of trades. But that goes to my daughters, who can't get along as well as I can because I have carefully raised them as young ladies, who don't know anything and can't do anything. I hope Congress will extend to them the charity which they have failed to get from me.

Why, if a man who is not even mad, but only strenuous—strenuous about race-suicide—should come to me and try to get me to use my large political and ecclesiastical influence to get a bill passed by this Congress limiting families to twenty-two children by one mother, I should try to calm him down. I should reason with him. I should say to him, "Leave it alone. Leave it alone and it will take care of itself. Only one couple a year in the United States can reach that limit. If they have reached that limit let them go right on. Let them have all the liberty they want. In restricting that family to twenty-two children you are merely conferring discomfort and unhappiness on one family per year in a nation of 88,000,000, which is not worth while."

It is the very same with copyright. One author per year produces a book which can outlive the forty-two-year limit; that's all. This nation can't produce two authors a year that can do it; the thing is demonstrably impossible. All that the limited copyright can do is to take the bread out of the mouths of the children of that one author per year.

I made an estimate some years ago, when I appeared before a committee of the House of Lords, that we had published in this country since the Declaration of Independence 220,000 books. They have all gone. They had all perished before they were ten years old. It is only one book in one thousand that can outlive the forty-two-year limit. Therefore why put a limit at all? You might as well limit the family to twenty-two children.

If you recall the Americans in the nineteenth century who wrote books that lived forty-two years you will have to begin with Cooper; you can follow with Washington Irving, Harriet Beecher Stowe, Edgar Allan Poe, and there you have to wait a long time. You come to Emerson, and you have to stand still and look further. You find Howells and T. B. Aldrich, and, then your numbers begin to run pretty thin, and you question if you can name twenty persons in the United States who in a whole century have written books that would live forty-two years. Why, you could take them all and put them on one bench there *[pointing]*. Add the wives and children and you could put the result on two or three more benches.

One hundred persons—that is the little, insignificant crowd whose bread-and-butter is to be taken away for what purpose, for what profit to anybody? You turn these few books into the hands of the pirate and of the legitimate publisher, too, and they get the profit that should have gone to the wife and children.

When I appeared before that committee of the House of Lords the chairman asked me what limit I would propose. I said, "Perpetuity." I could see some resentment in his manner, and he said the idea was illogical, for the reason that it has long ago been decided that there can be no such thing as property in ideas. I said there was property in ideas before Queen Anne's time; they had perpetual copyright. He said, "What is a book? A book is just built from base to roof on ideas, and there can be no property in it."

I said I wished he could mention any kind of property on this planet that had a pecuniary value which was not derived from an idea or ideas. He said real estate. I put a supposititious case, a dozen Englishmen who travel through South Africa and camp out, and eleven of them see nothing at all; they are mentally blind. But there is one in the party who knows what this harbor means and what the lay of the land means. To him it means that some day a railway will go through here, and there on that harbor a great city will spring up. That is his idea. And he has another idea, which is to go and trade his last bottle of Scotch whiskey and his last horse-blanket to the principal chief of that region and buy a piece of land the size of Pennsylvania. That was the value of an idea that the day would come when the Cape to Cairo Railway would be built.

Every improvement that is put upon the real estate is the result of an idea in somebody's head. The skyscraper is another idea; the railroad is another; the telephone and all those things are merely symbols which represent ideas. An andiron, a wash-tub, is the result of an idea that did not exist before.

So if, as that gentleman said, a book does consist solely of ideas, that is the best argument in the world that it is property, and should not be under any limitation at all. We don't ask for that. Fifty years from now we shall ask for it.

I hope the bill will pass without any deleterious amendments. I do seem to be extraordinarily interested in a whole lot of arts and things that I have got nothing to do with. It is a part of my generous, liberal nature; I can't help it. I feel the same sort of charity to everybody that was manifested by a gentleman who arrived at home at two o'clock in the morning from the club and was feeling so perfectly satisfied with life, so happy, and so comfortable, and there was his house weaving, weaving, weaving around. He watched his chance, and by-and-by when the steps got in his neighborhood he made a jump and climbed up and got on the portico.

And the house went on weaving and weaving and weaving, but he watched the door, and when it came around his way he plunged through it. He got to the stairs, and when he went up on all fours the house was so unsteady that he could hardly make his way, but at last he got to the top and raised his foot and put it on the top step. But only the toe hitched on the step, and he rolled down and fetched up on the bottom step, with his arm around the newel-post, and he said: "God pity the poor sailors out at sea on a night like this."

BOOKS, AUTHORS, AND HATS

London, June 25, 1907

Address at the Pilgrims' Club Luncheon, given in Twain's honor at the Savoy Hotel. He was introduced by Augustine Birrell, a member of Parliament and chief-secretary for Ireland.

Pilgrims, I desire first to thank those undergraduates of Oxford. When a man has grown so old as I am, when he has reached the verge of seventy-two years, there is nothing that carries him back to the dreamland of his life, to his boyhood, like recognition of those young hearts up yonder. And so I thank them out of my heart. I desire to thank the Pilgrims of New York also for their kind notice and message which they have cabled over here. Mr. Birrell says he does not know how he got here. But he will be able to get away all right—he has not drunk anything since he came here. I am glad to know about those friends of his, Otway and Chatterton—fresh, new names to me. I am glad of the disposition he has shown to rescue them from the evils of poverty, and if they are still in London, I hope to have a talk with them. For a while I thought he was going to tell us the effect which my book had upon his growing manhood. I thought he was going to tell us how much that effect amounted to, and whether it really made him what he now is, but with the discretion born of Parliamentary experience he dodged that, and we do not know now whether he read the book or not. He did that very neatly. I could not do it any better myself.

My books have had effects, and very good ones, too, here and there, and some others not so good. There is no doubt about that. But I remember one monumental instance of it years and years ago. Professor Norton, of Harvard, was over here, and when he came back to Boston I went out with Howells to call on him. Norton was allied in some way by marriage with Darwin. Mr. Norton was very gentle in what he had to say, and almost delicate, and he said: "Mr. Clemens, I have been spending some time with Mr. Darwin in England, and I should like to tell you something connected with that visit. You were the object

146

of it, and I myself would have been very proud of it, but you may not be proud of it. At any rate, I am going to tell you what it was, and to leave to you to regard it as you please. Mr. Darwin took me up to his bedroom and pointed out certain things there—pitcher-plants, and so on, that he was measuring and watching from day to day—and he said: 'The chambermaid is permitted to do what she pleases in this room, but she must never touch those plants and never touch those books on that table by that candle. With those books I read myself to sleep every night.' Those were your own books." I said: "There is no question to my mind as to whether I should regard that as a compliment or not. I do regard it as a very great compliment and a very high honor that that great mind, laboring for the whole human race, should rest itself on my books. I am proud that he should read himself to sleep with them."

Now, I could not keep that to myself—I was so proud of it. As soon as I got home to Hartford I called up my oldest friend—and dearest enemy on occasion—the Rev. Joseph Twichell, my pastor, and I told him about that, and, of course, he was full of interest and venom. Those people who get no compliments like that feel like that. He went off. He did not issue any applause of any kind, and I did not hear of that subject for some time. But when Mr. Darwin passed away from this life, and some time after Darwin's *Life and Letters* came out, the Rev. Mr. Twichell procured an early copy of that work and found something in it which he considered applied to me. He came over to my house—it was snowing, raining, sleeting, but that did not make any difference to Twichell. He produced the book, and turned over and over, until he came to a certain place, when he said: "Here, look at this letter from Mr. Darwin to Sir Joseph Hooker." What Mr. Darwin said—I give you the idea and not the very words—was this: I do not know whether I ought to have devoted my whole life to these drudgeries in natural history and the other sciences or not, for while I may have gained in one way I have lost in another. Once I had a fine perception and appreciation of high literature, but in me that quality is atrophied. "That was the reason," said Mr. Twichell, "he was reading your books."

Mr. Birrell has touched lightly—very lightly, but in not an uncomplimentary way—on my position in this world as a moralist. I am glad to have that recognition, too, because I have suffered since I have been in this town; in the first place, right away, when I came here, from a newsman going around with a great red, highly displayed placard in the place of an apron. He was selling newspapers, and there were two sentences on that placard which would have been all right if they had been punctuated; but they ran those two sentences together without a comma or anything, and that would naturally create a wrong impression, because it said, "Mark Twain Arrives Ascot Cup Stolen." No doubt many a person was misled by those sentences joined together in that unkind way. I have no doubt my character has suffered from it. I suppose I ought to defend my character, but how can I defend it? I can say here and now—and anybody can see by my face that I am sincere, that I speak the truth—that I have never seen that Cup. I have not got the Cup—I did not have a chance to get it. I have always had a good character in that way. I have hardly ever stolen anything, and if I did steal anything I had discretion enough to know about the value of it first. I do not steal things that are likely to get myself into trouble. I do not think any of us do that. I know we all take things—that is to be expected—but really, I have never taken anything, certainly in England, that amounts to any great thing. I do confess that when I was here seven years ago I stole a hat, but that did not amount to anything. It was not a good hat, and was only a clergyman's hat, anyway.

I was at a luncheon party, and Archdeacon Wilberforce was there also. I dare say he is Archdeacon now—he was a canon then—and he was serving in the Westminster battery, if that is the proper term—I do not know, as you mix military and ecclesiastical things together so much. He left the luncheon table before I did. He began this. I did steal his hat, but he began by taking mine. I make that interjection because I would not accuse Archdeacon Wilberforce of stealing my hat—I should not think of it. I confine that phrase to myself. He merely took my hat. And with good judgment, too—it was a better hat than his. He came out before the luncheon was over, and sorted the hats in the hall, and selected one which suited. It happened to be mine. He went off with it. When I came out by-and-by there was no hat there which would go on my head except his, which was left behind. My head was not the customary size just at that time. I had been receiving a good many very nice and complimentary attentions, and my head was a couple of sizes larger than usual, and his hat just suited me. The bumps and corners were all right intellectually. There were results pleasing to me—possibly so to him. He found out whose hat it was, and wrote me saying it was pleasant that all the way home, whenever he met anybody his gravities, his solemnities, his deep thoughts, his eloquent remarks were all snatched up by the people he met, and mistaken for brilliant humorisms.

I had another experience. It was not unpleasing. I was received with a deference which was entirely foreign to my experience by everybody whom I met, so that before I got home I had a much higher opinion of myself than I have ever had before or since. And there is in that very connection an incident which I remember at that old date which is rather melancholy to me, because it shows how a person can deteriorate in a mere seven years. It is seven years ago. I have not that hat now. I was going down Pall-Mall, or some other of your big streets, and I recognized that that hat needed ironing. I went into a big shop and passed in my hat, and asked that it might be ironed. They were courteous, very courteous, even courtly. They brought that hat back to me presently very sleek and nice, and I asked how much there was to pay. They replied that they did not charge the clergy anything. I have cherished the delight of that moment from that day to this. It was the first thing I did the other day to go and hunt up that shop and hand in my hat to have it ironed. I said when it came back, "How much to pay?" They said, "Ninepence." In seven years I have acquired all that worldliness, and I am sorry to be back where I was seven years ago.

But now I am chaffing and chaffing and chaffing here, and I hope you will forgive me for that; but when a man stands on the verge of seventy-two you know perfectly well that he never reached that place without knowing what this life is—heartbreaking bereavement. And so our reverence is for our dead. We do not forget them; but our duty is toward the living; and if we can be cheerful, cheerful in spirit, cheerful in speech and in hope, that is a benefit to those who are around us.

My own history includes an incident which will always connect me with England in a pathetic way, for when I arrived here seven years ago with my wife and my daughter—we had gone around the globe lecturing to raise money to clear off a debt—my wife and one of my daughters started across the ocean to bring to England our eldest daughter. She was twenty-four years of age and in the bloom of young womanhood, and we were unsuspecting. When my wife and daughter—and my wife has passed from this life since—when they had reached mid-Atlantic, a cablegram—one of those heartbreaking cablegrams which we all in our days have to experience—was put into my hand. It stated that that daughter of ours had gone to her long sleep. And so, as I say, I cannot always be cheerful, and I cannot always be chaffing; I must sometimes lay the cap and bells aside, and recognize that I am of the human race like the rest, and must have my cares and griefs. And therefore I noticed what Mr. Birrell said—I was so glad to hear him say it—something that was in the nature of these verses here at the top of this:

> He lit our life with shafts of sun
>   And vanquished pain.
> Thus two great nations stand as one
>   In honoring Twain.

I am very glad to have those verses. I am very glad and very grateful for what Mr. Birrell said in that connection. I have received since I have been here, in this one week, hundreds of letters from all conditions of people in England—men, women, and children—and there is in them compliment, praise, and, above all and better than all, there is in them a note of affection. Praise is well, compliment is well, but affection—that is the last and final and most precious reward that any man can win, whether by character or achievement, and I am very grateful to have that reward. All these letters make me feel that here in England—as in America—when I stand under the English flag, I am not a stranger. I am not an alien, but at home.

THE DAY WE CELEBRATE (II)

London, July 4, 1907

The American Society in London gave an Independence Day banquet at the Hotel Cecil. Joseph Choate called on Twain to respond to the toast "The Day We Celebrate."

Mr. Chairman, My Lord, and Gentlemen,

Once more it happens, as it has happened so often since I arrived in England a week or two ago, that instead of celebrating the Fourth of July properly as has been indicated, I have to first take care of my personal character.

Sir Mortimer Durand still remains unconvinced. Well, I tried to convince these people from the beginning that I did not take the Ascot Cup; and as I have failed to convince anybody that I did not take the cup, I might as well confess I did take it and be done with it. I don't see why this uncharitable feeling should follow me everywhere, and why I should have that crime thrown up to me on all occasions. The tears that I have wept over it ought to have created a different feeling than this—and, besides, I don't think it is very right or fair that, considering England has been trying to take a cup of ours for forty years—I don't see why they should take so much trouble when I tried to go into the business myself.

Sir Mortimer Durand, too, has had trouble from going to a dinner here, and he has told you what he suffered in consequence. But what did he suffer? He only missed his train and one night of discomfort, and he remembers it to this day. Oh! if you could only think what I have suffered from a similar circumstance. Two or three years ago, in New York, with that Society there which is made up of people from all British Colonies, and from Great Britain, generally, who were educated in British colleges and British schools, I was there to respond to a toast of some kind or other, and I did then what I have been in the habit of doing, from a selfish motive, for a long time, and that is, I got myself placed No. 3 in the list of speakers—then you get home early.

I had to go five miles up-river, and had to catch a particular train or not get there. But see the magnanimity which is born in me, which I have cultivated all my life. A very famous and very great British clergyman came to me presently, and he said: "I am away down in the list; I have got to catch a certain train this Saturday night; if I don't catch that train I shall be carried beyond midnight and break the Sabbath. Won't you change places with me?"

I said: "Certainly I will." I did it at once. Now, see what happened. Talk about Sir Mortimer Durand's sufferings for a single night! I have suffered ever since. because I saved that gentleman from breaking the Sabbath—yes, saved him. I took his place, but I lost my train, and it was I who broke the Sabbath. Up to that time I never had broken the Sabbath in my life and from that day to this I never have kept it.

Oh! I am learning much here tonight. I find I didn't know anything about the American Society—that is, I didn't know its chief virtue. I didn't know its chief virtue until his Excellency our Ambassador revealed it—I may say, exposed it. I was intending to go home on the 13th of this month, but I look upon that in a different light now. I am going to stay here until the American Society pays my passage.

Our Ambassador has spoken of our Fourth of July and the noise it makes. We have got a double Fourth of July—a daylight Fourth and a midnight Fourth. During the day in America, as our Ambassador has indicated, we keep the Fourth of July properly in a reverent spirit. We devote it to teaching our children patriotic things—reverence for the Declaration of Independence. We honor the day all through the daylight hours, and when night comes we dishonor it. Presently—before long—they are getting nearly ready to begin now—on the Atlantic coast, when night shuts down, that pandemonium will begin, and there will be noise, and noise, and noise—all night long—and there will be more than noise—there will be people crippled, there will be people killed, there will be people who will lose their eyes, and all through that permission which we give to irresponsible boys to play with firearms and fire-crackers, and all sorts of dangerous things. We turn that Fourth of July, alas! over to rowdies to drink and get drunk and make the night hideous, and we cripple and kill more people than you would imagine.

We probably began to celebrate our Fourth-of-July night in that way one hundred and twenty-five years ago, and on every Fourth-of-July night since these horrors have grown and grown, until now, in our five thousand towns of America, somebody gets killed or crippled on every Fourth-of-July night, besides those cases of sick persons whom we never hear of, who die as the result of the noise or the shock. They cripple and kill more people on the Fourth of July in America than they kill and cripple in our wars nowadays, and there are no pensions for these folk. And, too, we burn houses. Really we destroy more property on every Fourth-of-July night than the whole of the United States was worth one hundred and twenty-five years ago. Really our Fourth of July is our day of mourning, our day of sorrow. Fifty thousand people who have lost friends, or who have had friends crippled, receive that Fourth of July, when it comes, as a day of mourning for the losses they have sustained in their families.

I have suffered in that way myself. I have had relatives killed in that way. One was in Chicago years ago—an uncle of mine, just as good an uncle as I have ever had, and I had lots of them—yes, uncles to burn, uncles to spare. This poor uncle, full of patriotism, opened his mouth to hurrah, and a rocket went down his throat. Before that man could ask for a drink of water to quench that thing, it blew up and scattered him all over the forty-five States, and—really, now, this is true—I know about it myself-twenty-four hours after that it was raining buttons, recognizable as his, on the Atlantic seaboard. A person cannot have a disaster like that and be entirely cheerful the rest of his life. I had another uncle, on an entirely different Fourth of July, who was blown up that way, and really it trimmed him as it would a tree. He had hardly a limb left on him anywhere. All we have left now is an expurgated edition of that uncle. But never mind about these things; they are merely passing matters. Don't let me make you sad.

Sir Mortimer Durand said that you, the English people, gave up your colonies over there—got tired of them—and did it with reluctance. Now I wish you just to consider that he was right about that, and that he had his reasons for saying that England did not look upon our Revolution as a foreign war, but as a civil war fought by Englishmen.

Our Fourth of July which we honor so much, and which we love so much, and which we take so much pride in, is an English institution, not an American one, and it comes of a great ancestry. The first Fourth of July in that noble genealogy dates back seven centuries lacking eight years. That is the day of the Great Charter—the Magna Charta—which was born at Runnymede in the next to the last year of King John, and portions of the liberties secured thus by those hardy Barons from that reluctant King John are a part of our Declaration of Independence, of our Fourth of July, of our American liberties. And the second of those Fourths of July was not born until four centuries later, in Charles the First's time in the Bill of Rights, and that is ours, that is part of our liberties. The next one was still English, in New England, where they established that principle which remains with us to this day, and in will continue to remain with us—no taxation without representation. That is always going to stand, and that the English Colonies in New England gave us.

The Fourth of July, and the one which you are celebrating now, born in Philadelphia on the 4th of July, 1776—that is English, too. It is not American. Those were English colonists, subjects of King George III, Englishmen at heart, who protested against the oppressions of the Home Government. Though they proposed to cure those oppressions and remove them, still remaining under the Crown, they were not intending a revolution. The revolution was brought about by circumstances which they could not control. The Declaration of Independence was written by a British subject, every name signed to it was the name of a British subject. There was not the name of a single American attached to the Declaration of Independence—in fact, there was not an American in the country in that day except the Indians out on the plains. They were Englishmen, all Englishmen—Americans did not begin until seven years later, when that Fourth of July had become seven years old, and then the American Republic was established. Since then there have been Americans. So you see what we owe to England in the matter of liberties.

We have, however, one Fourth of July which is absolutely our own, and that is that great proclamation issued forty years ago by that great American to whom Sir Mortimer Durand paid that just and beautiful tribute—Abraham Lincoln. Lincoln's proclamation, which not only set the black slaves free, but set the white man free also. The owner was set free from the burden and offence, that sad condition of things where he was in so many instances a master and owner of slaves when he did not want to be. That proclamation set them all free. But even in this matter England suggested it, for England had set her slaves free thirty years before, and we followed her example. We always followed her example, whether it was good or bad.

And it was an English judge that issued that other great proclamation, and established that great principle that, when a slave, let him belong to whom he may, and let him come whence he may, sets his foot upon English soil, his fetters by that act fall away and he is a free man before the world. We followed the example of 1833, and we freed our slaves as I have said.

It is true, then, that all our Fourths of July, and we have five of them, England gave to us, except that one that I have mentioned—the Emancipation Proclamation, and, lest we forget, let us all remember that we owe these things to England. Let us be able to say to Old England, this great-hearted, venerable old mother of the race, you gave us our Fourths of July that we love and that we honor and revere, you gave us the Declaration of Independence, which is the Charter of our rights, you, the venerable Mother of Liberties, the Protector of Anglo-Saxon Freedom— you gave us these things, and we do most honestly thank you for them.

THE SAVAGE CLUB DINNER

London, July 6, 1907

The members of the Savage Club presented Twain with his portrait. In the toast "The Health of Mark Twain," a member described reading some of Twain's work to Harold Frederic during Frederic's fatal illness.

Mr. Chairman and Fellow-Savages,

I am very glad indeed to have that portrait. I think it is the best one that I have ever had, and there have been opportunities before to get a good photograph. I have sat to photographers twenty-two times today. Those sittings added to those that have preceded them since I have been in Europe—if we average at that rate—must have numbered one hundred to two hundred sittings. Out of all those there ought to be some good photographs. This is the best I have had, and I am glad to have your honored names on it.

I did not know Harold Frederic personally, but I have heard a great deal about him, and nothing that was not pleasant and nothing except such things as lead a man to honor another man and to love him. I consider that it is a misfortune of mine that I have never had the luck to meet him, and if any book of mine read to him in his last hours made those hours easier for him and more comfortable, I am very glad and proud of that.

I call to mind such a case many years ago of an English authoress, well known in her day, who wrote such beautiful child tales, touching and lovely in every possible way. In a little biographical sketch of her I found that her last hours were spent partly in reading a book of mine, until she was no longer able to read. That has always remained in my mind, and I have always cherished it as one of the good things of my life. I had read what she had written, and had loved her for what she had done.

[The explorer Henry M.] Stanley apparently carried a book of mine feloniously away to Africa, and I have not a doubt that it had a noble and uplifting influence there in the wilds of Africa—because on his

155

previous journeys he never carried anything to read except Shakespeare and the Bible. I did not know of that circumstance. I did not know that he had carried a book of mine. I only noticed that when he came back he was a reformed man. I knew Stanley very well in those old days. Stanley was the first man who ever reported a lecture of mine, and that was in St. Louis. When I was down there the next time to give the same lecture I was told to give them something fresh, as they had read that in the papers. I met Stanley here when he came back from that first expedition of his which closed with the finding of Livingstone. You remember how he would break out at the meetings of the British Association, and find fault with what people said, because Stanley had notions of his own, and could not contain them. They had to come out or break him up—and so he would go round and address geographical societies. He was always on the war-path in those days, and people always had to have Stanley contradicting their geography for them and improving it. But he always came back and sat drinking beer with me in the hotel up to two in the morning, and he was then one of the most civilized human beings that ever was.

I saw in a newspaper this evening a reference to an interview which appeared in one of the papers the other day, in which the interviewer said that I characterized Mr. Birrell's speech the other day at the Pilgrims' Club as "bully." Now, if you will excuse me, I never use slang to an interviewer or anybody else. That distresses me. Whatever I said about Mr. Birrell's speech was said in English, as good English as anybody uses. If I could not describe Mr. Birrell's delightful speech without using slang I would not describe it at all. I would close my mouth and keep it closed, much as it would discomfort me.

Now that comes of interviewing a man in the first person, which is an altogether wrong way to interview him. It is entirely wrong because none of you, I, or anybody else, could interview a man—could listen to a man talking any length of time and then go off and reproduce that talk in the first person. It can't be done. What results is merely that the interviewer gives the substance of what is said and puts it in his own language and puts it in your mouth. It will always be either better language than you use or worse, and in my case it is always worse. I have a great respect for the English language. I am one of its supporters, its promoters, its elevators. I don't degrade it. A slip of the tongue would be the most that you would get from me. I have always tried hard and faithfully to improve my English and never to degrade it. I always try to use the best English to describe what I think and what I feel, or what I don't feel and what I don't think.

I am not one of those who in expressing opinions confine themselves to facts. I don't know anything that mars good literature so completely as too much truth. Facts contain a deal of poetry, but you can't use too many of them without damaging your literature. I love all literature, and as long as I am a doctor of literature—I have suggested to you for twenty years I have been diligently trying to improve my own literature, and now, by virtue of the University of Oxford, I mean to doctor everybody else's.

Now I think I ought to apologize for my clothes. At home I venture things that I am not permitted by my family to venture in foreign parts. I was instructed before I left home and ordered to refrain from white clothes in England. I meant to keep that command fair and clean, and I would have done it if I had been in the habit of obeying instructions, but I can't invent a new process in life right away. I have not had white clothes on since I crossed the ocean until now.

In these three or four weeks I have grown so tired of gray and black that you have earned my gratitude in permitting me to come as I have. I wear white clothes in the depth of winter in my home, but I don't go out in the streets in them. I don't go out to attract too much attention. I like to attract some, and always I would like to be dressed so that I may, be more conspicuous than anybody else.

If I had been an ancient Briton, I would not have contented myself with blue paint, but I would have bankrupted the rainbow. I so enjoy gay clothes in which women clothe themselves that it always grieves me when I go to the opera to see that, while women look like a flower-bed, the men are a few gray stumps among them in their black evening dress. These are two or three reasons why I wish to wear white clothes. When I find myself in assemblies like this, with everybody in black clothes, I know I possess something that is superior to everybody else's. Clothes are never clean. You don't know whether they are clean or not, because you can't see.

Here or anywhere you must scour your head every two or three days or it is full of grit. Your clothes must collect just as much dirt as your hair. If you wear white clothes you are clean, and your cleaning bill gets so heavy that you have to take care. I am proud to say that I can wear a white suit of clothes without a blemish for three days. If you need any further instruction in the matter of clothes I shall be glad to give it to you. I hope I have convinced some of you that it is just as well to wear white clothes as any other kind. I do not want to boast. I only want to make you understand that you are not clean.

As to age, the fact that I am nearly seventy-two years old does not clearly indicate how old I am, because part of every day—it is with me as with you—you try to describe your age, and you cannot do it. Sometimes you are only fifteen; sometimes you are twenty-five. It is very seldom in a day that I am seventy-two years old. I am older now sometimes than I was when I used to rob orchards; a thing which I would not do today—if the orchards were watched. I am so glad to be here tonight. I am so glad to renew with the Savages that now ancient time when I first sat with a company of this club in London in 1872. That is a long time ago. But I did stay with the Savages a night in London long ago, and as I had come into a very strange land, and was with friends, as I could see, that has always remained in my mind as a peculiarly blessed evening, since it brought me into contact with men of my own kind and my own feelings.

I am glad to be here, and to see you all again, because it is very likely that I shall not see you again. It is easier than I thought to come across the Atlantic. I have been received, as you know, in the most delightfully generous way in England ever since I came here. It keeps me choked up all the time. Everybody is so generous, and they do seem to give you such a hearty welcome. Nobody in the world can appreciate it higher than I do. It did not wait till I got to London, but when I came ashore at Tilbury the stevedores on the dock raised the first welcome—a good and hearty welcome from the men who do the heavy labor in the world, and save you and me having to do it. They are the men who with their hands build empires and make them prosper. It is because of them that the others are wealthy and can live in luxury. They received me with a "Hurrah!" that went to my heart. They are the men that build civilization, and without them no civilization can be built. So I came first to the authors and creators of civilization, and I blessedly end this happy meeting with the Savages who destroy it.

ROBERT FULTON DAY

Jamestown, Virginia, September 23, 1907

At the Virginia exposition, Virginia's Lieutenant-Governor James Taylor Ellyson introduced Twain. After much applause, Twain spoke.

Ladies and Gentlemen,

I am but human, and when you give me a reception like that I am obliged to wait a little while I get my voice. When you appeal to my head, I don't feel it; but when you appeal to my heart, I do feel it.

We are here to celebrate one of the greatest events of American history, and not only in American history, but in the world's history.

Indeed it was—the application of steam by Robert Fulton.

It was a world event—there are not many of them. It is peculiarly an American event, that is true, but the influence was very broad in effect. We should regard this day as a very great American holiday. We have not many that are exclusively American holidays. We have the Fourth of July, which we regard as an American holiday, but it is nothing of the kind. I am waiting for a dissenting voice. All great efforts that led up to the Fourth of July were made, not by Americans, but by English residents of America, subjects of the King of England.

They fought all the fighting that was done, they shed and spilt all the blood that was spilt, in securing to us the invaluable liberties which are incorporated in the Declaration of Independence; but they were not Americans. They signed the Declaration of Independence; no American's name is signed to that document at all. There never was an American such as you and I are until after the Revolution, when it had all been fought out and liberty secured, after the adoption of the Constitution, and the recognition of the Independence of America by all powers.

While we revere the Fourth of July—and let us always revere it, and the liberties it conferred upon us—yet it was not an American event, a great American day.

It was an American who applied that steam successfully. There are not a great many world events, and we have our full share. The telegraph, telephone, and the application of steam to navigation—these are great American events.

Today I have been requested, or I have requested myself, not to confine myself to furnishing you with information, but to remind you of things, and to introduce one of the nation's celebrants.

Admiral [Purnell Frederick] Harrington here is going to tell you all that I have left untold. I am going to tell you all that I know, and then he will follow up with such rags and remnants as he can find, and tell you what he knows.

No doubt you have heard a great deal about Robert Fulton and the influences that have grown from his invention, but the little steamboat is suffering neglect.

You probably do not know a great deal about that boat. It was the most important steamboat in the world. I was there and saw it. Admiral Harrington was there at the time. It need not surprise you, for he is not as old as he looks. That little boat was interesting in every way. The size of it. The boat was one *[consults Admiral]*, he said ten feet long. The breadth of that boat *[consults Admiral]*, two hundred feet. You see, the first and most important detail is the length, then the breadth, and then the depth; the depth of that boat was *[consults again]*—the Admiral says it was a flat boat. Then her tonnage—you know nothing about a boat until you know two more things: her speed and her tonnage. We know the speed she made. She made four miles—and sometimes five miles. It was on her initial trip, on August 11, 1807, that she made her initial trip, when she went from *[consults Admiral]* Jersey City—to Chicago. That's right. She went by way of Albany. Now comes the tonnage of that boat. Tonnage of a boat means the amount of displacement; displacement means the amount of water a vessel can shove in a day. The tonnage of man is estimated by the amount of whiskey he can displace in a day.

Robert Fulton named the *Clermont* in honor of his bride, that is, Clermont was the name of the county-seat.

I feel that it surprises you that I know so much. In my remarks of welcome of Admiral Harrington I am not going to give him compliments. Compliments always embarrass a man. You do not know anything to say. It does not inspire you with words. There is nothing you can say in answer to a compliment. I have been complimented myself a great many times, and they always embarrass me—I always feel that they have not said enough.

The Admiral and myself have held public office, and were associated together a great deal in a friendly way in the time of Pocahontas.

That incident where Pocahontas saves the life of Smith from her father Powhatan's club was gotten up by the Admiral and myself to advertise Jamestown.

At that time the Admiral and myself did not have the facilities of advertising that you have.

I have known Admiral Harrington in all kinds of situations—in public service, on the platform, and in the chain-gang now and then—but it was a mistake. A case of mistaken identity. I do not think it is at all a necessity to tell you Admiral Harrington's public history. You know that it is in the histories. I am not here to tell you anything about his public life, but to expose his private life.

I am something of a poet. When the great poet laureate, Tennyson, died, and I found that the place was open, I tried to get it—but I did not get it. Anybody can write the first line of a poem, but it is a very difficult task to make the second line rhyme with the first. When I was down in Australia there were two towns named Johnswood and Par-am. I made this rhyme:

> The people of Johnswood are pious and good;
> The people of Par-am they don't care a—

I do not want to compliment Admiral Harrington, but as long as such men as he devote their lives to the public service the credit of the country will never cease. I will say that the same high qualities, the same moral and intellectual attainments, the same graciousness of manner, of conduct, of observation, and expression have caused Admiral Harrington to be mistaken for me—and I have been mistaken for him.

A mutual compliment can go no further, and I now have the honor and privilege of introducing to you Admiral Harrington.

THE ALPHABET AND SIMPLIFIED SPELLING

New York City, December 9, 1907

Andrew Carnegie was honored at the dedication of the Associated Societies of Engineers club. Twain was introduced by T. C. Martin, who mentioned an incident from Twain's unpublished autobiography.

It seems to me that I was around here in the neighborhood of the Public Library about fifty or sixty years ago. I don't deny the circumstance, although I don't see how you got it out of my autobiography, which was not to be printed until I am dead, unless I'm dead now. I had that $3 in change, and I remember well the $10 which was sewed in my coat. I have prospered since. Now I have plenty of money and a disposition to squander it, but I can't. One of those trust companies is taking care of it.

Now, as this is probably the last time that I shall be out after nightfall this winter, I must say that I have come here with a mission, and I would make my errand of value.

Many compliments have been paid to Mr. Carnegie tonight. I was expecting them. They are very gratifying to me.

I have been a guest of honor myself, and I know what Mr. Carnegie is experiencing now. It is embarrassing to get compliments and compliments and only compliments, particularly when he knows as well as the rest of us that on the other side of him there are all sorts of things worthy of our condemnation.

Just look at Mr. Carnegie's face. It is fairly scintillating with fictitious innocence. You would think, looking at him, that he had never committed a crime in his life. But no—look at his pestiferous simplified spelling. You can't any of you imagine what a crime that has been. Torquemada was nothing to Mr. Carnegie. That old fellow shed some blood in the Inquisition, but Mr. Carnegie has brought destruction to the entire race. I know he didn't mean it to be a crime, but it was, just the same. He's got us all so we can't spell anything.

The trouble with him is that he attacked orthography at the wrong end. He meant well, but he attacked the symptoms and not the cause of the disease. He ought to have gone to work on the alphabet. There's not a vowel in it with a definite value, and not a consonant that you can hitch anything to. Look at the "h's" distributed all around. There's "gherkin." What are you going to do with the "h" in that? What the devil's the use of "h" in gherkin, I'd like to know. It's one thing I admire the English for: they just don't mind anything about them at all.

But look at the "pneumatics" and the "pneumonias" and the rest of them. A real reform would settle them once and for all, and wind up by giving us an alphabet that we wouldn't have to spell with at all, instead of this present silly alphabet, which I fancy was invented by a drunken thief. Why, there isn't a man who doesn't have to throw out about fifteen hundred words a day when he writes his letters because he can't spell them! It's like trying to do a St. Vitus's dance with wooden legs.

Now I'll bet there isn't a man here who can spell "pterodactyl," not even the prisoner at the bar. I'd like to hear him try once—but not in public, for it's too near Sunday, when all extravagant histrionic entertainments are barred. I'd like to hear him try in private, and when he got through trying to spell "pterodactyl" you wouldn't know whether it was a fish or a beast or a bird, and whether it flew on its legs or walked with its wings. The chances are that he would give it tusks and make it lay eggs.

Let's get Mr. Carnegie to reform the alphabet, and we'll pray for him—if he'll take the risk.

If we had adequate, competent vowels, with a system of accents, giving to each vowel its own soul and value, so every shade of that vowel would be shown in its accent, there is not a word in any tongue that we could not spell accurately. That would be competent, adequate, simplified spelling, in contrast to the clipping, the hair punching, the carbuncles, and the cancers which go by the name of simplified spelling. If I ask you what *b-o-w* spells you can't tell me unless you know which *b-o-w* I mean, and it is the same with *r-o-w, b-o-r-e,* and the whole family of words which were born out of lawful wedlock and don't know their own origin.

Now, if we had an alphabet that was adequate and competent, instead of inadequate and incompetent, things would be different. Spelling reform has only made it bald-headed and unsightly. There is the whole tribe of them, "row" and "read" and "lead"–a whole family who don't know who they are. I ask you to pronounce *s-o-w,* and you ask me what kind of a one.

If we had a sane, determinate alphabet, instead of a hospital of com-minuted eunuchs, you would know whether one referred to the act of a man casting the seed over the ploughed land or whether one wished to recall the lady hog and the future ham.

It's a rotten alphabet. I appoint Mr. Carnegie to get after it, and leave simplified spelling alone. Simplified spelling brought about sun-spots, the San Francisco earthquake, and the recent business depression, which we would never have had if spelling had been left all alone.

Now, I hope I have soothed Mr. Carnegie and made him more com-fortable than he would have been had he received only compliment after compliment, and I wish to say to him that simplified spelling is all right, but, like chastity, you can carry it too far.

GENERAL MILES AND THE DOG

New York City, December 22, 1907

As the guest of honor at Pleiades Club dinner at the Hotel Brevoort, the toast-master Carter Cole, Howells (or F.A. Nast) writes, "introduced [Twain] with a high tribute to his place in American literature, saying that he was dear to the hearts of all Americans."

It is hard work to make a speech when you have listened to compliments from the powers in authority. A compliment is a hard text to preach to. When the chairman introduces me as a person of merit, and when he says pleasant things about me, I always feel like answering simply that what he says is true; that it is all right; that, as far as I am concerned, the things he said can stand as they are. But you always have to say something, and that is what frightens me.

I remember out in Sydney once having to respond to some complimentary toast, and my one desire was to turn in my tracks like any other worm—and run for it. I was remembering that occasion at a later date when I had to introduce a speaker. Hoping, then, to spur his speech by putting him, in joke, on the defensive, I accused him in my introduction of everything I thought it impossible for him to have committed. When I finished there was an awful calm. I had been telling his life history by mistake.

One must keep up one's character. Earn a character first if you can, and if you can't, then assume one. From the code of morals I have been following and revising and revising for seventy-two years I remember one detail. All my life I have been honest—comparatively honest. I could never use money I had not made honestly—I could only lend it.

Last spring I met General Miles again, and he commented on the fact that we had known each other thirty years. He said it was strange that we had not met years before, when we had both been in Washington. At that point I changed the subject, and I changed it with art. But the facts are these:

165

I was then under contract for my *Innocents Abroad*, but did not have a cent to live on while I wrote it. So I went to Washington to do a little journalism. There I met an equally poor friend, William Davidson, who had not a single vice, unless you call it a vice in a Scot to love Scotch. Together we devised the first and original newspaper syndicate, selling two letters a week to twelve newspapers and getting $1 a letter. That $24 a week would have been enough for us—if we had not had to support the jug.

But there was a day when we felt that we must have $3 right away— $3 at once. That was how I met the General. It doesn't matter now what we wanted so much money at one time for, but that Scot and I did occasionally want it. The Scot sent me out one day to get it. He had a great belief in Providence, that Scottish friend of mine. He said: "The Lord will provide."

I had given up trying to find the money lying about, and was in a hotel lobby in despair, when I saw a beautiful unfriended dog. The dog saw me, too, and at once we became acquainted. Then General Miles came in, admired the dog, and asked me to price it. I priced it at $3. He offered me an opportunity to reconsider the value of the beautiful animal, but I refused to take more than Providence knew I needed. The General carried the dog to his room.

Then came in a sweet little middle-aged man, who at once began looking around the lobby.

"Did you lose a dog?" I asked. He said he had.

"I think I could find it," I volunteered, "for a small sum."

"How much?" he asked. And I told him $3. He urged me to accept more, but I did not wish to outdo Providence. Then I went to the General's room and asked for the dog back. He was very angry, and wanted to know why I had sold him a dog that did not belong to me.

"That's a singular question to ask me, sir," I replied. "Didn't you ask me to sell him? You started it." And he let me have him. I gave him back his $3 and returned the dog, collect, to its owner. That second $3 I carried home to the Scot, and we enjoyed it, but the first $3, the money I got from the General, I would have had to lend.

The General seemed not to remember my part in that adventure, and I never had the heart to tell him about it.

ROGERS AND RAILROADS

Norfolk, Virginia, April, 3, 1909

In celebration of the opening of the Virginian Railway, a group of Norfolk businessmen honored Henry H. Rogers, the chief supporter of the railroad. Twain expressed his gratitude for Rogers's past encouragement and also paid tribute to Helen Keller.

I thank you, Mr. Toastmaster, for the compliment which you have paid me, and I am sure I would rather have made people laugh than cry, yet in my time I have made some of them cry; and before I stop entirely I hope to make some more of them cry. I like compliments. I deal in them myself. I have listened with the greatest pleasure to the compliments which the chairman has paid to Mr. Rogers and that road of his tonight, and I hope some of them are deserved.

It is no small distinction to a man like that to sit here before an intelligent crowd like this and to be classed with Napoleon and Caesar. Why didn't he say that this was the proudest day of his life? Napoleon and Caesar are dead, and they can't be here to defend themselves. But I'm here!

The chairman said, and very truly, that the most lasting thing in the hands of man are the roads which Caesar built, and it is true that he built a lot of them; and they are there yet.

Yes, Caesar built a lot of roads in England, and you can find them. But Rogers has only built one road, and he hasn't finished that yet. I like to hear my old friend complimented, but I don't like to hear it overdone.

I didn't go around today with the others to see what he is doing. I will do that in a quiet time, when there is not anything going on, and when I shall not be called upon to deliver intemperate compliments on a railroad in which I own no stock.

They proposed that I go along with the committee and help inspect that dump down yonder. I didn't go, I saw that dump. I saw that thing when I was coming in on the steamer, and I didn't go because I was diffident, sentimentally diffident, about going and looking at that thing again—that great, long, bony thing; it looked just like Mr. Rogers's foot.

The chairman says Mr. Rogers is full of practical wisdom, and he is. It is intimated here that he is a very ingenious man, and he is a very competent financier. Maybe he is now, but it was not always so. I know lots of private things in his life which people don't know, and I know how he started; and it was not a very good start. I could have done better myself.

The first time he crossed the Atlantic he had just made the first little strike in oil, and he was so young he did not like to ask questions. He did not like to appear ignorant. To this day he don't like to appear ignorant, but he can look as ignorant as anybody. On board the ship they were betting on the run of the ship, betting a couple of shillings, or half a crown, and they proposed that this youth from the oil regions should bet on the run of the ship. He did not like to ask what a half-crown was, and he didn't know; but rather than be ashamed of himself he did bet half a crown on the run of the ship, and in bed he could not sleep. He wondered if he could afford that outlay in case he lost. He kept wondering over it, and said to himself: "A king's crown must be worth $20,000, so half a crown would cost $10,000." He could not afford to bet away $10,000 on the run of the ship, so he went up to the stakeholder and gave him $150 to let him off.

I like to hear Mr. Rogers complimented. I am not stingy in compliments to him myself. Why, I did it today when I sent his wife a telegram to comfort her. That is the kind of person I am. I knew she would be uneasy about him. I knew she would be solicitous about what he might do down here, so I did it to quiet her and to comfort her. I said he was doing well for a person out of practice. There is nothing like it. He is like I used to be. There were times when I was careless—careless in my dress when I got older.

You know how uncomfortable your wife can get when you are going away without her superintendence. Once when my wife could not go with me (she always went with me when she could—I always did meet that kind of luck), I was going to Washington once, a long time ago, in Mr. Cleveland's first administration, and she could not go; but, in her anxiety that I should not desecrate the house, she made preparation. She knew that there was to be a reception of those authors at the White House at seven o'clock in the evening. She said, "If I should tell you now what I want to ask of you, you would forget it before you get to Washington, and, therefore, I have written it on a card, and you will find it in your dress-vest pocket when you are dressing at the Arlington—when you are dressing to see the President." I never thought of it again until I was dressing, and I felt in that pocket and took it out, and it said, in a kind of imploring way, "Don't wear your arctics in the White House."

You complimented Mr. Rogers on his energy, his foresightedness, complimented him in various ways, and he has deserved those compliments, although I say it myself; and I enjoy them all. There is one side of Mr. Rogers that has not been mentioned. If you will leave that to me I will touch upon that. There was a note in an editorial in one of the Norfolk papers this morning that touched upon that very thing, that hidden side of Mr. Rogers, where it spoke of Helen Keller and her affection for Mr. Rogers, to whom she dedicated her life book. And she has a right to feel that way, because, without the public knowing anything about it, he rescued, if I may use that term, that marvelous girl, that wonderful Southern girl, that girl who was stone deaf, blind, and dumb from scarlet-fever when she was a baby eighteen months old; and who now is as well and thoroughly educated as any woman on this planet at twenty-nine years of age. She is the most marvelous person of her sex that has existed on this earth since Joan of Arc.

That is not all Mr. Rogers has done; but you never see that side of his character, because it is never protruding; but he lends a helping hand daily out of that generous heart of his. You never hear of it. He is supposed to be a moon which has one side dark and the other bright. But the other side, though you don't see it, is not dark; it is bright, and its rays penetrate, and others do see it who are not God.

I would take this opportunity to tell something that I have never been allowed to tell by Mr. Rogers, either by my mouth or in print, and if I don't look at him I can tell it now.

In 1893, when the publishing company of Charles L. Webster, of which I was financial agent, failed, it left me heavily in debt. If you will remember what commerce was at that time you will recall that you could not sell anything, and could not buy anything, and I was on my back; my books were not worth anything at all, and I could not give away my copyrights. Mr. Rogers had long enough vision ahead to say, "Your books have supported you before, and after the panic is over they will support you again," and that was a correct proposition. He saved my copyrights, and saved me from financial ruin. He it was who arranged with my creditors to allow me to roam the face of the earth for four years and persecute the nations thereof with lectures, promising that at the end of four years I would pay dollar for dollar. That arrangement was made; otherwise I would now be living out-of-doors under an umbrella, and a borrowed one at that.

You see his white mustache and his head trying to get white (he is always trying to look like me—I don't blame him for that). These are only emblematic of his character, and that is all. I say, without exception, hair and all, he is the whitest man I have ever known.

DOVER · THRIFT · EDITIONS

NONFICTION

POETICS, Aristotle. (0-486-29577-X)

MEDITATIONS, Marcus Aurelius. (0-486-29823-X)

THE WAY OF PERFECTION, St. Teresa of Avila. Edited and Translated by E. Allison Peers. (0-486-48451-3)

THE DEVIL'S DICTIONARY, Ambrose Bierce. (0-486-27542-6)

THE UNITED STATES CONSTITUTION: THE FULL TEXT WITH SUPPLEMENTARY MATERIALS, Edited and with supplementary materials by Bob Blaisdell. (0-486-47166-7)

GREAT SPEECHES BY NATIVE AMERICANS, Edited by Bob Blaisdell. (0-486-41122-2)

GREAT SPEECHES OF THE 20TH CENTURY, Edited by Bob Blaisdell. (0-486-47467-4)

INFAMOUS SPEECHES: FROM ROBESPIERRE TO OSAMA BIN LADEN, Edited by Bob Blaisdell. (0-486-47849-1)

THE COMMUNIST MANIFESTO AND OTHER REVOLUTIONARY WRITINGS: MARX, MARAT, PAINE, MAO TSE-TUNG, GANDHI AND OTHERS, Edited by Bob Blaisdell. (0-486-42465-0)

GREAT ENGLISH ESSAYS: FROM BACON TO CHESTERTON, Edited by Bob Blaisdell. (0-486-44082-6)

GREAT INAUGURAL ADDRESSES, Edited by James Daley. (0-486-44577-1)

GREAT SPEECHES ON GAY RIGHTS, Edited by James Daley. (0-486-47512-3)

GREAT SPEECHES BY AMERICAN WOMEN, Edited by James Daley. (0-486-46141-6)

GREAT SPEECHES BY AFRICAN AMERICANS: FREDERICK DOUGLASS, SOJOURNER TRUTH, DR. MARTIN LUTHER KING, JR., BARACK OBAMA, AND OTHERS, Edited by James Daley. (0-486-44761-8)

ON THE ORIGIN OF SPECIES: BY MEANS OF NATURAL SELECTION, Charles Darwin. (0-486-45006-6)

NARRATIVE OF THE LIFE OF FREDERICK DOUGLASS, Frederick Douglass. (0-486-28499-9)

THE SOULS OF BLACK FOLK, W. E. B. DuBois. (0-486-28041-1)

NATURE AND OTHER ESSAYS, Ralph Waldo Emerson. (0-486-46947-6)

SELF-RELIANCE AND OTHER ESSAYS, Ralph Waldo Emerson. (0-486-27790-9)

THE LIFE OF OLAUDAH EQUIANO, Olaudah Equiano. (0-486-40661-X)

THE AUTOBIOGRAPHY OF BENJAMIN FRANKLIN, Benjamin Franklin. (0-486-29073-5)

WIT AND WISDOM FROM POOR RICHARD'S ALMANACK, Benjamin Franklin. (0-486-40891-4)

Browse over 9,000 books at www.doverpublications.com

DOVER · THRIFT · EDITIONS

DOVER·THRIFT·EDITIONS

FICTION

FLATLAND: A ROMANCE OF MANY DIMENSIONS, Edwin A. Abbott. (0-486-27263-X)

SHORT STORIES, Louisa May Alcott. (0-486-29063-8)

EMMA, Jane Austen. (0-486-40648-2)

PRIDE AND PREJUDICE, Jane Austen. (0-486-28473-5)

SENSE AND SENSIBILITY, Jane Austen. (0-486-29049-2)

THE UNKNOWN MASTERPIECE AND OTHER STORIES, Honore de Balzac. (0-486-40649-0)

CIVIL WAR STORIES, Ambrose Bierce. (0-486-28038-1)

CIVIL WAR SHORT STORIES AND POEMS, Edited by Bob Blaisdell. (0-486-48226-X)

THE DECAMERON: SELECTED TALES, Giovanni Boccaccio. Edited by Bob Blaisdell. (0-486-41113-3)

JANE EYRE, Charlotte Brontë. (0-486-42449-9)

WUTHERING HEIGHTS, Emily Brontë. (0-486-29256-8)

THE THIRTY-NINE STEPS, John Buchan. (0-486-28201-5)

ALICE'S ADVENTURES IN WONDERLAND, Lewis Carroll. (0-486-27543-4)

PAUL'S CASE AND OTHER STORIES, Willa Cather. (0-486-29057-3)

MY ÁNTONIA, Willa Cather. (0-486-28240-6)

O PIONEERS!, Willa Cather. (0-486-27785-2)

FAVORITE FATHER BROWN STORIES, G. K. Chesterton. (0-486-27545-0)

THE RIDDLE OF THE SANDS, Erskine Childers. (0-486-40879-5)

THE AWAKENING, Kate Chopin. (0-486-27786-0)

LORD JIM, Joseph Conrad. (0-486-40650-4)

HEART OF DARKNESS, Joseph Conrad. (0-486-26464-5)

THE LAST OF THE MOHICANS, James Fenimore Cooper. (0-486-42678-5)

THE OPEN BOAT AND OTHER STORIES, Stephen Crane. (0-486-27547-7)

THE RED BADGE OF COURAGE, Stephen Crane. (0-486-26465-3)

THE WORLD'S GREATEST SHORT STORIES, Edited by James Daley. (0-486-44716-2)

ROBINSON CRUSOE, Daniel Defoe. (0-486-40427-7)

OLIVER TWIST, Charles Dickens. (0-486-42453-7)

A TALE OF TWO CITIES, Charles Dickens. (0-486-40651-2)

GREAT EXPECTATIONS, Charles Dickens. (0-486-41586-4)

HARD TIMES, Charles Dickens. (0-486-41920-7)

DOVER · THRIFT · EDITIONS

DOVER·THRIFT·EDITIONS

DOVER · THRIFT · EDITIONS

AROUND THE WORLD IN EIGHTY DAYS, Jules Verne. (0-486-41111-7)

CANDIDE, Voltaire. Edited by Francois-Marie Arouet. (0-486-26689-3)

GREAT SHORT STORIES BY AMERICAN WOMEN, Edited by Candace Ward. (0-486-28776-9)

THE INVISIBLE MAN, H. G. Wells. (0-486-27071-8)

THE TIME MACHINE, H. G. Wells. (0-486-28472-7)

THE WAR OF THE WORLDS, H. G. Wells. (0-486-29506-0)

THE COUNTRY OF THE BLIND: AND OTHER SCIENCE-FICTION STORIES, H. G. Wells. Edited by Martin Gardner. (0-486-48289-8)

ETHAN FROME, Edith Wharton. (0-486-26690-7)

THE AGE OF INNOCENCE, Edith Wharton. (0-486-29803-5)

THE PICTURE OF DORIAN GRAY, Oscar Wilde. (0-486-27807-7)

MONDAY OR TUESDAY: EIGHT STORIES, Virginia Woolf. (0-486-29453-6)

DAISY MILLER, Henry James. (0-486-28773-4)

DAVID COPPERFIELD, Charles Dickens. (0-486-43665-9)

DUBLINERS, James Joyce. (0-486-26870-5)

EMMA, Jane Austen. (0-486-40648-2)

THE GIFT OF THE MAGI AND OTHER SHORT STORIES, O. Henry. (0-486-27061-0)

THE GOLD-BUG AND OTHER TALES, Edgar Allan Poe. (0-486-26875-6)

GREAT SHORT SHORT STORIES, Edited by Paul Negri. (0-486-44098-2)

GULLIVER'S TRAVELS, Jonathan Swift. (0-486-29273-8)

HARD TIMES, Charles Dickens. (0-486-41920-7)

THE HOUND OF THE BASKERVILLES, Arthur Conan Doyle. (0-486-28214-7)

THE ILIAD, Homer. (0-486-40883-3)

MOBY-DICK, Herman Melville. (0-486-43215-7)

MY ÁNTONIA, Willa Cather. (0-486-28240-6)

NORTHANGER ABBEY, Jane Austen. (0-486-41412-4)

NOT WITHOUT LAUGHTER, Langston Hughes. (0-486-45448-7)

OLIVER TWIST, Charles Dickens. (0-486-42453-7)

PERSUASION, Jane Austen. (0-486-29555-9)

THE PHANTOM OF THE OPERA, Gaston Leroux. (0-486-43458-3)

A PORTRAIT OF THE ARTIST AS A YOUNG MAN, James Joyce. (0-486-28050-0)

PUDD'NHEAD WILSON, Mark Twain. (0-486-40885-X)